Diary of a fan
An eventful season (and a half)
A personal account of the second spell of Kenny Dalglish as Liverpool FC manager

Pablo Gutiérrez

Ediciones La Catedral y La Colina
Madrid

Copyright © 2012 by Pablo Gutiérrez

All rights reserved. No part of this book may be reproduced in any manner whatsoever without written permission except in the case of brief quotations embodied in critical articles and reviews. For information, contact the author at pgflfc@hotmail.com

ISBN: 978-1478161127

Contents

PROLOGUE 7

INTRODUCTION.- An eventful season (and a half) 11

SECOND HALF OF SEASON 2010/2011 17
   1.- A win and a Spearing hope 19
   2.- Suarez-sational, Dalglashtic 21
   3.- Understanding King Kenny 24
   4.- A couple of not so terrible defeats 28
   5.- Some questions looking for answer 32
   6.- That one-man team issue 34
   7.- A football less weekend 38
   8.- Difficult to find words 42
   9.- Regularity and brilliance 46
   10.- Magical thinking, logical thinking 51
   11.- Goals for fun 55
   12.- The definite proof 59
   13.- Can such a thing as a "blessing in disguise" really exist? 63

SEASON 2011/2012 67
   14.- Football again 69
   15.- The foundations for the success 72
   16.- The many halves in a glass 77
   17.- Defining moments 81
   18.- Youth of today 86
   19.- Game-planning and team-comparing 90
   20.- First and second units tested 95
   21.- Einstein and balanced assessment 99
   22.- Looking for theories 104
   23.- Learning curve 108

24.- The same old story, same old act	112
25.- Back to basics	116
26.- Year ending, year beginning	121
27.- Charming players	126
28.- The way forward	130
29.- Eight games later	135
30.- A spell cast on the opposite goal	140
31.- Ability and will	145
32.- Performance marking	150
33.- Young derbies, youth system	155
34.- Winning titles, playing football	160
35.- Some disconnected thoughts	165
36.- Luck and lessons to learn	169
37.- Creative anger	174
38.- Movement, mobility	179
39.- Walking through a storm	184
40.- A drop of golden sun	189
41.- A second drop	193
42.- Loyalty, pragmatism, fantasies	197
43.- Match and Cup lost; player and team gained?	201
44.- Unfinished business	205
45.- End of a season, end of an era	209

PROLOGUE

I began to write a blog about Liverpool Football Club with no further plans besides letting my opinions known to other LFC fans who might be interested. Thus, the first version of almost all articles included in this book was uploaded to the social network of the club website. However, what began almost as a joke to myself evolved, and more or less suddenly I realised that I had written tens of entries to the blog, amounting several thousands of words.

Words that had developed, unconsciously, into some kind of a narrative of LFC seasons as they were unfolding. Maybe it would be of interest for any fan to have all this articles gathered? Difficult to know, but probably it was worth trying. A book looked a good solution, provided the process of publishing could be no excessively time and money consuming. With that in mind, the ebook offered a perfect match for my needs at the moment.

Thus, I decided that I was going to give it a go. All of the entries, as a whole, summed up my personal views, from the perspective of an LFC fan, of how season 11/12, and the second part of season 10/11, unfolded. I discuss some aspects of LFC matches, and sometimes also some aspects of football in general. While my intention was to write after every match, at least Premier League matches, the reality was that I was not always able to write, so there are some voids.

I have opted for keeping the entries more or less unchanged. I have edited and corrected some mistakes (English not being my first language, I am aware that many mistakes remain, and I only hope that the texts can be understood, and not too annoying for the readers), and added a bit of context, in the form of the date in which the article was written and the results of the first team since the previous article, to help the reader; when a particular article refers to matches from other LFC teams, those results are also included. But, other than those minor adjustments, rewriting the texts would risk losing the character of a proper "diary", that should be written as the days pass by, not altogether after all is concluded. Likewise, adding now some entries that were missing at the time for lack of time (or inspiration) would also mean somewhat of a trick, benefiting from hindsight that may have altered the perceptions of the moment.

So here the reader will find my honest views at the given moments. There are also voids, in the weeks I was not able to write. Most conspicuously, as you will see, at the beginning of season 2011/2012, in which it took time for me to start posting.

In some cases the reality has proven me blatantly wrong; in other cases, I was fairly right. In the majority, I was neither wrong nor right. During the season, I have changed, or adjusted, my own views at times, as can be seen from the succession of articles. After all, offering some food for thought and reflection is the main target when speaking about football issues. I tried to add some wider football views, not only a view of the matches themselves, so my hope is that these articles might have something to say even after the season.

Coincidence has determined that these articles cover, more or less, the length of the second spell of Dalglish at Anfield bench. It was not intentional, but the articles began shortly after "The return of the king"; and obviously the season ended with his dismissal. In between, almost 18 months full of both, joy and despair, for LFC fans. But a time, I think, worth remembering.

I thank all the website users who took time to read and/or comment on the first versions of these posts. The chance to debate and discuss have always been interesting and enjoyable.

Should any reader wish to contact me with their personal opinions, views, ideas, agreements or disagreements, etc., I will be very happy to hear from you at pgflfc@hotmail.com.

One (or two) last question remains unanswered: Is this all worth it? Will there be anybody out there who may be interested in what has become nothing more (and nothing less) than a personal account of the second spell of Dalglish as LFC manager? I am about to find out.

INTRODUCTION.- An eventful season (and a half)

2011/2012 might have been a disappointing season, league wise, for LFC; but, as a whole, it would be difficult to think of it as a dull, boring, season. There has been something of almost everything, from blatant below par performances and results to great moments of football and scores; from the return of a legend as manager for a complete season to the sacking of the same legend; from achieving the lowest position in league table for fifty years to adding silverware to Anfield cabinet for the first time in six years; from one of the main players serving an eight-match ban to going to Wembley no less than three times;...A really eventful season.

It was a season that saw Dalglish come back and go; Carragher falling down the pecking order; Gerrard unable to play as many matches as we all would have wanted; Leiva injured for the best part of the season; a third-choice goal-keeper figuring in an all Merseyside Wembley FA Cup semi-final due to red cards in consecutive matches for two goal-keepers.

The single character that will most probably preside over the season as a whole is Kenny Dalglish. The King came back to the rescue of a team in difficult circumstances on January 2011. He steered the team to a more than fitting end of 2010/2011 season, achieving 34 points in 18 league games and falling only a little bit short of getting an European qualification. Mission fully accomplished regarding the end of the season, including the replacement of Torres and Babel with Suarez and Carroll during January transfer window.

After such a promising end of the season, Dalglish was appointed manager, and things appeared to bode well for 2011/12. Not that everything went perfectly on that final months of 2010/11 season; but, overall, the positives clearly outweighed the negatives. On the one hand, the team was at times unreliable, with significant spells of below par performances; the European campaign was disappointing, and the team couldn't make it to a European competition for 2011/12 season; the new signing Carroll didn't quite achieve the level that was expected. On the other hand, the points tally was clearly improved over the first half of the season; the team improved at given times, with some good displays, and moments of great goal scoring records; Suarez took the league by storm, scoring, assisting, and creating all sorts of problems to opposition defences. Hence, with a projection of more than 70 points over a whole season, Dalglish confirmed as a manager, things getting better on and off the field, and at least two clear fields in which to improve (recovering the best playing form from Carroll, and making adjustments to the squad in the transfer window), new season looked promising.

If winter transfer window had been relevant, summer window was extremely busy, with signings and outings galore. A total of seven players arrived (Jose Enrique, Adam, Henderson, Downing, Bellamy, Coates, Doni) in an attempt to reignite the club. However, the team quickly started to show what ultimately proved to be a persistent trend during the season. Good games, bad games; good results, bad results; good news, bad news;…and so on.

Inconsistency has been a major trait for LFC during the season.

Inconsistency, that is, except in cup games. FA Cup and League Cup campaigns have been extremely consistent; oddly enough, the draws have determined that all rounds in the FA Cup have been at home and all rounds in the League Cup have been away from home. All the same, LFC were able to convincingly get to both finals and prove that the current squad is capable of not only winning against any other given team, but also winning deservedly while being the better team on the pitch.

At the same time, though, LFC proved also, in league games, that they were capable of losing against almost any other team, and losing clearly while being outplayed. In all truth, it is also the case that in some games the final score was not what was deserved. Especially in games at Anfield, the team deserved more points than achieved, and at times it seemed almost impossible not to have won certain matches.

The squad needed to recover from two tough setbacks near the end of 2011. During the Carling Cup Chelsea game (by the way: it is worth mentioning that, in the space of 10 days, LFC won not once, but twice, in the home of the future Champions of Europe), Leiva sustained an injury that was going to keep him out of the team for the rest of the season. Shortly after, Suarez got an eight-match ban on the grounds of alleged racist behaviour towards Evra. Needless to say, much was written and spoken about the issue, and the team needed to endure a difficult period; not only because of having to compete without arguably its best player, but also because all the talking about the incident.

However, LFC managed more or less to keep going during the suspension, and the definite dip in form came after the returning of Suarez. To what extent that period of bad results had something to do with the Suarez affair, and what would have been the situation had it not been for it, is something we will never know for sure. But those were, at the very least, hard times for anyone involved in LFC affairs.

Once the league form collapsed since February, the team focused on adding the FA Cup to the Carling Cup, won on penalty shoot-out against Cardiff. First piece of silverware coming into Anfield cabinet in six years, and the undisputable highest point of the season for LFC. The last matches of the season saw LFC languishing in the league table while two good pieces of news reached Anfield: the surge in form of Andy Carroll, that started to show the abilities that convinced LFC sign him, and the team getting to the FA Cup final, meaning a third trip to Wembley in the campaign.

FA Cup final was narrowly lost, and the league season finished with LFC equalling their lowest position in the table since the returning to the first division under Bill Shankly (third time to finish 8th in 50 years) and the single lowest amount of points during a season since the Premier League started.

Obviously, the cups campaigns have been more that satisfactory for a team still in the process of rebuilding, and the League Cup title and three trips to Wembley have reinvigorated the Anfield fans. However, the league form, the "bread and butter" competition for LFC, has been hugely disappointing, and the owners made a controversial decision, equally highly contested and widely supported, and parted company with Kenny Dalglish, putting an end to a 18-month long second tenure by The King.

18 months full of highs and lows, of joy and despair, of optimism and pessimism. 18 months that marked the farewell to one of the biggest Anfield legends. 18 months after which one more trophy rests in Anfield. Those are the 18 eventful months surveyed in the following pages.

SECOND HALF OF SEASON 2010/2011

1.- *A win and a Spearing hope*

Date: 1-March-2011
Previous results: LFC 1-0 Sparta Prague (UEFA Europa League); West Ham 3-1 LFC (Premier League); LFC Reserves 2-0 Blackburn Reserves

While I wasn't in the mood of writing about our Sparta Prague match, I am much less keen to write the West Ham one. Back to the bad times of Hodgson, bad times of Benitez, bad times of Houllier,...(I am not going as back as Evans). A team without soul, without belief,...Better players than West Ham's but, as of Sunday, worse team. Let's hope King Kenny can fix the situation.

But there was an LFC win this week. For the Reserves, Monday night, against Blackburn. Not a win in the mould of U18's, but a convincing win. That feeling of being a better team even not playing at full capacity. Being much better, it is often not necessary to have a great match, and that was the case with the Reserves against Blackburn.

And there was this Spearing hope. I for one am getting more and more convinced that Jay Spearing should be given a real go at the first team. I mean, let him be the core of the team, let him dictate the match. He is by far the closest we have in the squad to Xabi Alonso. He is not quit as good, but at least he has in him some of the qualities needed. And we cannot afford to let those qualities count only for the Reserves. They must be tested in first team action.

He can pass the ball, both short and long (and, also important and often overview, to middle distances, where lots of passes are lost every match by LFC players). He has an eye for a pass through defences. He can cover a great deal of the pitch. Mind you, I am not saying he is Pele. He is not Alonso, either. But what he lacks the most to fulfil his own potential is rhythm (he needs to do the things he does with much less time and space) and deep knowledge of that role. The kind of knowledge Alonso has, not only because his quality, but also because he has been playing there for 10, 15 years. That provides you with several invaluable resources, instinctive reactions, intuition,…

So what Spearing lacks can only be achieved if he is given a string of first team matches in which he can develop his own capacities. At the very least, we would know, by the end of the season, if he is a proper LFC player or not, if he is really useful as a squad member. On the other hand, if he keeps on playing the odd game, we will always suspect what he is, or is not, capable of, but we will never know for sure.

He may not be LFC level (I hope he is, but it isn't easy to be sure), but one thing I know: neither Leiva nor Poulsen can do that job. They can be good servants, they can be useful, but they cannot boss a football match from the ball.

Well, that is my hope. To see Spearing in a consistent run with the first team. Should he prove unable to fulfill the requirements, at least he would have had his fair chance. He deserves it.

I really looking forward to posting after a good LFC match. If only it were next weekend...

2.- *Suarez-sational, Dalglashtic*

Date: 9-March-2011
Previous results: LFC 3-1 Man United (Premier League)

It's been a few days now since that magic Sunday, and that gives a little perspective, which is good for writing (to be honest, that is not the reason I have not posted before; I simply couldn't for a variety of reasons, but lets take the perspective approach).

Clearly, that perspective doesn't change in the slightest what is the great news: what a player we have signed in Suarez! Don't get me wrong: it's great to have a win over ManU. But the really great news for the future is the confirmation of what many in and out the club suspected: Suarez is a top, top class player. On TV one of the pundits even said that not even Messi would have been able to make that first goal movement, between 3,4,5 defences with nearly no space, using both legs,...A joy to watch.

Still, it is worth saying that Sunday match was a team effort of great level. I think Gerrard has not got as much praise as he deserved. He totally bossed the game from the midfield, and should have scored with those two efforts near the end. Kuyt of course did all that one should expect from a front man, not only getting a hat trick but also pressing the defenders, and offering space and alternatives for his team-mates to play.

Meireles, maybe a little bit less participative than in previous matches, was always there for getting the ball and giving it back: take, pass, move, as goes a very dear motto. Carragher was excellent, both at center back and at right back (excluding that action with Nani that should have been avoided).

Skrtel and Kirgiakos gave a good account of themselves, both pretty solid, and it was a pity they couldn't keep their focus in that last moment in which ManU got their goal. Johnson was good when he had to occupy the Aurelio place in the left side. Although was even better at the beginning at the right side. Maxi and Lucas worked well, and were always on hand to help the play, and keep the ball going. Mmmm...someone missing? Yes, Reina hardly needed to do anything, in what is a great testimony to the solidity of the team.

But I think that what stood out was the master game plan. Kenny Dalglish, Steve Clarke, and Sammy Lee (and whoever else took part in it) deserve a lot of credit. They absolutely outplayed ManU. Everybody had thought about the weakness in the centre of the ManU defence, with Ferdinand, Vidic and Evans absent. But the way in which Liverpool took advantage of it was nothing sort of genius.

Instead of going directly to the centre, the players made the pitch wide, with Suarez and Kuyt both on the flanks. Smalling and Brown didn't even have a player on sight to defend against. The Liverpool players gained space on the flanks (thus preventing Rafael and Evra from helping his team mates) and from there went to the centre with all the advantage to their side. The ManU centre-backs hardly knew what to do, how to face this clearly unexpected challenge.

Sir Alex was unable to solve this problem. The game plan set up by the Liverpool staff worked perfectly and left ManU players in absolute despair and helpless. Liverpool had a game plan, and the players knew exactly what to do in each situation. ManU went into the game with no idea of what was going to happen to them, and couldn't respond whatsoever.

So, great team performance, brilliantly designed by the technical staff and developed by the players, and an outstanding player in Suarez. Not bad combination for a winning team. And a certain Carroll showing what he is capable of.
Let's hope the team can show some regularity from now.

It's been a joy to write this post. See you after Braga match.

3.- Understanding King Kenny

Date: 11-March-2011
Previous results: Sporting Braga 1-0 LFC (UEFA Europa League)

Another very bad performance against SC Braga left us (at least left me) pondering what to make of this team. The string of great, mediocre, bad, good,...matches is intriguing, and resists any intended analysis. This has been a constant during this season. Even under Roy Hodgson there were some really great matches (West Ham at home, Tottenham away, to name only two examples) combined with some really awful ones (I bet I don't need to give you examples). Same goes under Dalglish, apparently.

After a great performance on Sunday, with a lot of well deserved praise for Dalglish and the players, we found ourselves facing a really, really poorly played match. Very similar to West Ham away, or Sparta de Prague, or many others. How could a team experience such a dramatic change in just a few days? What should we expect from the season from now on? Is there any way of shedding some light on the issue of the extent of the rebuilding needed? Do we need, as some say, "two or three" new players to be again a real force? Or do we need an almost complete revamp of the squad?

If you have kept reading until here hoping for an answer, I am afraid I am going to disappoint you. I am as lost as the next guy. Moreover, I seriously doubt that anybody could answer those questions. The team is inconsistent, and desperately need to gain more reliability. I honestly haven't seen ManU playing great football this season. But they can somehow drag results even so. That was also true for LFC two, three seasons ago. And it needs to be true for us again, although we most probably will need to wait at least until next season. The rest of 10/11 campaign (9 league games, and between 1 and 6 Europe League games) is going to be as intriguing as it has been until know. We will probably watch some great matches, and, as likely as not, we are going to watch some very bad performances. At least, it gives you an invaluable feeling of uncertainty and emotion prior to the games.

Meanwhile, I for one have difficulties in understanding some of the squad selection decisions. Regarding Braga game:

- I strongly believe that Carragher is more or less as good as left back as he is as right back. And obviously Johnson is much better as right back. So, why not swap sides? I can understand playing Johnson as left back in an emergency situation, or if Kelly is really much better at right side than at left side (which I don't really know). But, once you are playing with Carragher and Johnson, it would make much more sense to me playing Johnson at right and Carragher at left. OK, it worked well during the ManU game, after Aurelio left. But still.

- What are we waiting for to give a real chance to Pacheco? We need to know if he is a useful Liverpool player or not. He needs to grow, to experience first team action. So these Europe League matches look perfect for both purposes. And I don't mean throwing him to the pitch for the last 10 minutes of a game. I am sure he wouldn't have played worse than Poulsen last night.

- Spearing as right midfielder, even as right wing? Well, I can take it as a try. But it was deemed to fail. By the way, I would like to say that the improvement in the team after Carroll was on the pitch was due mainly to Carroll, no doubt about that. But also to Spearing playing as central midfielder, which meant much better ball control and circulation. He made some mistakes, too, but I think he played well there.

This is not to imply anything negative about Dalglish. I was quick to sing his praises in my last post, and there is probably a reason behind those decisions, but I would like to know it. There were also positives last night. One that comes to mind is Andy Carroll, which simply by being on the pitch changed the match. But I also think that Joe Cole, while not close to his brilliant best, showed some signs of improvement and real commitment to the team. He may be a valuable addition to the squad if he can stay injury-free. Spearing played fine at central midfield, as said before. And the result, as Dalglish himself has said, was not as bad as it could have been. There is still hope for next week. And much more for the Premier League, with Suarez in the team.

One final confession, just on the light side: I don't only have difficulties understanding some of King Kenny's team selection. Also in understanding him in a more literal way. I am obviously not an English native speaker, but all LFC managers in "Internet era" (that is, Houllier, Benitez and Hodgson) spoke as clearly as one would want. I could listen to any interview, or press conference, and completely understand them. With Dalglish…well, let say that is not exactly the case. I struggle to understand him, and I get frustrated when hearing all the laughing in his press conferences while I have not been able to get the joke. On the plus side, given enough time I will be able to visit Glasgow without help. Long live the King.

Finally, here is to a great U18 win next Sunday.

4.- A couple of not so terrible defeats

Date: 18- March-2011
Previous results: LFC U18 2-3 Man United U18; Arsenal Reserves 2-1 LFC Reserves

When I started posting here, my self-imposed aim was (and still is) to post as frequently as possible after LFC games, to give my personal thoughts on the team. So I should be writing now about last night match against SC Braga. But…I have opted for allowing myself a little bit of additional time after so disappointing a match. Also, I have a strong interest in Academy football, so, in the meantime, I will write about last developments on that front.

First, our Youth Cup game against ManU. Clearly a disappointing outcome, with the Borrell team out of the Cup. Still, a lot of positives to be proud of. While the match remained 'normal' our team proved to be much better. Not as brilliant as in another matches, but the opposition was way stronger. Anyway, LFC dominated the game, imposed the tempo, created the better chances, and found themselves 2-0 up shortly after halftime. At that moment everything was pointing to a comfortable win.

However, when things started to get unusual, after the penalty and the red cards, our players seemed to completely lose control of the actions. Not that ManU was by any means a better team, but they showed more composure, and with the help of Lady Luck (which is something we are used to, coming from them), they ran out winners much to the despair of the 10.000 (aren't we the best fans in the world?) LFC supporters at Anfield for a Youth Cup quarter-final.

That meant that the Youth Cup run came to an abrupt end. But this team has made us dream. Arguably the best matches by any LFC team this season have come from them. Not only there are bright prospects in that squad (Flanagan, Suso, Sterling, to name just a few) but they are also a great football team, with a clear idea of the way to play. Rodolfo Borrell has proved to be an outstanding manager, and his pre and post match interviews are a definite must. Not in the King Kenny mould, but in his own way: clear, straight-forward, brief statements from which a football fan can learn a lot. Our kids couldn't be in better hands.

Turning now to the other defeat, that of the reserves against Arsenal last Tuesday. Again, a disappointing ending, yet not totally discouraging display. LFC certainly started the match poorly, unable to progress on the pitch and always on their own half. Not that Arsenal showed great superiority, but they were clearly the better team. Had it not been for that penalty shot that hit the post, the game would have been all but finished by halftime, and with LFC hardly having started to play.

But things were totally different in the second half. I once heard a pundit saying that the work of a manager is best seen in the first ten minutes of the second half, when the players still remember the team talk. If that statement is anywhere near the reality, Pep Segura must be a great manager. The team looked totally different, and took the game to Arsenal. They only lacked the well deserved equaliser that only came in the final stages. A draw seemed a fair outcome, with each team having been better during one half.

The late Arsenal winner came as a blow. But the team and the recently appointed manager can learn a lot, both from the first half negatives and from the second half positives. Firstly, the team managed to sail through a bad performance and keep the match alive. After that, the team came out of nowhere to give a good account of themselves without getting the goal they deserved until very late...only to concede the defeat.

Let's hope Pep Segura can guide the players to a more consistent performance in the next miniderby and the rest of games ahead. A couple of final notes on the players. Tom Ince looks a nice prospect, but he needs to dramatically improve his finishing. He has shown both with the reserves and the U18 that he can run with the ball, he can beat defenders, he can link up with his team mates. But he seems to crack down in front of goal. (And yes, I am aware that he scored against Arsenal).

And a mention to one personal favourite, Michael Roberts. He is not spectacular, and he will hardly make the big headlines. But he is a very needed type of player, moving the ball, keeping it in play, bringing his team mates into play, opening spaces...As of today, he lacks consistency, he doesn't impose his seal on the games, he doesn't really boss the midfield, but hopefully, if given enough games and guidance, he will sort it out, and become a great player.

So this is it for the youngsters, which are having a much better season than the first team. I hope I will be posting on the first team shortly, if I find something to say.

5.- Some questions looking for answer

Date: 19-March-2011
Previous results: LFC 0-0 Sporting Braga (UEFA Europa League)

Can I offer a new perspective on the SC Braga match? I don't know, but at the very least I can try. Much has been written about that match. Which is a testimony to the commitment of The Kop, given that one is normally not very keen on reflecting on such a disappointing match.

Following that example, I have decided to also produce and honour my own aim of posting as often as possible after a first team match. As of now, there are no new things to tell about the match itself, so I will try to give you some occasion to think about this game. In two fields: language, and game management.

As for language, I honestly don't think my English teachers taught me a suitable word to qualify the performance on Tuesday night. The first leg again Sparta Praga was arguably awful; the second leg, maybe horrible, even if we won. The first leg again Braga, abysmal (that is with the help of a dictionary). But that second leg against Braga...I don't even know whether there is an appropriate word for it. Really, I hardly remember any similar display by any football team. Even worse given that opposition didn't pose much of a challenge. And a real challenge it is for my English.

As for game management, there is a trait in the way King Kenny manage the matches that I cannot honestly understand. Not that it is in some way to blame for the outcome of Braga match. Almost any LFC line-up should have been able to give a much better account of themselves. But still, I don't really understand the substitution policy.

Bear in mind that after a really badly played match, in which a goal was needed during all the game, Dalglish didn't even make the three changes. That I find difficult to understand. Surely some of the bench players might, at least theoretically, have been able to help improve the quality of play. And definitely there was not much risk of worsening it, was it? Besides that, it is not the first time that happens, I think. And usually almost every substitution comes at the late stages of the matches. Can it have to do with some type of "old school" way of handing matches? Or maybe with the staff lacking confidence in the rest of players?

Wouldn't it have been a good opportunity to at least allow Pacheco to give some indication of what he can do for the team? Or maybe King Kenny thought that introducing a young player in that context might have resulted in him losing confidence and effectively making things more difficult for him?

As you can see, today I have much more questions than answers. I hope tomorrow game will leave us with much more positive things to discuss about the team. Could that much anticipated partnership Suarez-Carroll start producing from the beginning?

6.- That one-man team issue

Date: 24-March-2011
Previous results: Sunderland 0-2 LFC (Premier League)

My post-Sunderland views are long overdue, now. After what was a good (but not exceptional) performance, with Suarez head and shoulders above any other player on the pitch, I was left thinking of an old debate many of you surely remember.

For many a year, LFC supporters had to suffer the constant references (and in this context they were more accusations than mere references) to the team being a one-man team or, at most, a two-man team. Those one/two being, of course, Gerrard and/or Torres. No matter what the statistics said, no matter the evidences, that label remained. Liverpool went on to win the Champions League, the FA Cup, the Community Shield, the European Supercup, to reach the second spot in the Premier League,...and, in some people's eyes, all of that could have been achieved with only Gerrard and Torres on the pitch.

After years in which the fans were fighting that theory, and arguing against it, what happened after the 2009 summer pointed to the fact that LFC was indeed a one-man team. That one man being...Xabi Alonso. His transfer brought down all the team balance. Sometimes it happens. A football team is often a very delicate machine, a set of different pieces, everyone dependant on the others, and the lacking of one single piece might have devastating effects on the machine as a whole. But it is not always easy to identify which piece cannot be replaced.

That is to say that we will never know what would have happen if Xabi would have stayed but Reina, or Gerrard, or Carragher, or Torres, or Mascherano, or Kuyt,…would have left. Maybe LFC was a one-man team only in the sense that every player was instrumental to the success. Maybe almost every player was 'the' one man. But it was Xabi who left, and the team never fully recovered.

During that 2008/2009 season LFC was arguably the best team in the Premier League, and I have few doubts that it should have won the title. It wasn't to be, though. However, everything was looking bright at that stage. The following season (2009/2010) would surely be 'our' season. We only needed that last step, and against an ageing Chelsea, a diminished ManU, an always-almost-but-never-ready Arsenal, the times ahead looked promising.

Then it came the summer of 2009, the transfer of Xabi, the lack of funds, the owners forgetting about the team, the team starting to get lost,…and the 'one-man team' became the no-man team, which is far worse. Confronted with a hostile environment inside the club, Rafa couldn't turn things around in the first post-Xabi season. We will never know for certain whether or not the sacking of Benitez was a wise movement, but Roy Hodgson couldn't fix the situation either.

So here we are, with King Kenny trying to rebuild the team while at the same team dragging the results to keep the team going. There have not been a great improvement in the performances of the team; still, the amount of Premier League points amassed (20 from 10 games as opposite to 25 from 20 games under Hodgson) allows for certain optimism.

However, both the direct watching of the games and what we have seen in the Europe League matches make the case for a one-man team tag revival. I can hardly remember one single player having so great an impact over a team display than the case with Suarez and LFC team nowadays. What seemed a hopeless team against Braga at Anfield (and in the first leg in Braga, and both matches against Sparta Praga) turns into a sparking and composed team when facing far better teams like ManU or Sunderland. And the one main (not only) difference is Luis Suarez.

So, is this a case of "here we go again, a one-man team"? Or is it just one stage in the rebuilding process? Or simply a player at his peak? Or a lack of depth in the squad? Remember that not many time ago the one man seemed to be Meireles, who is now almost irrelevant.

Anyway, Suarez was great against Sunderland, although we should not forget the contribution from Jay Spearing. He is not the best midfielder in the world, but he is a real midfielder. He is got a sense of where to go, what to do, when to wait and see and when to push forward,...He can find a team-mate with the ball, and make the circulation more steady. I think the team looks better with him.

Having said all that, the match against Sunderland was only a decent one. Until the penalty incident, the team looked mediocre, below Sunderland which were more likely to score. But credit to LFC players, they knew how to capitalise on the chance given and, after the 1-0, Sunderland never seemed even near to score. And that is a really good sign. If the team can keep improving the consistency in the games ahead, and maybe add a little bit of flair and class, we may end the season in a high and go into next summer in good mood after all.

As for the one-man team label, at this moment Suarez is clearly the main pillar of the team. I am looking forward to the development of his partnership with Carroll. Then we can move one step forward to being an eleven-man team, and a 25-man squad (well, this is too ambitious, but who knows?).

7.- *A football less weekend*

Date: 29-March-2011
Previous results: Everton Reserves 2-2 LFC Reserves; LFC U18 2-4 Nottingham Forest U18

An Argentine writer once said that there is nothing as absurd as a Sunday without football. Sunday is obviously the day in which most of league games are played in Argentina, so the same would apply to a weekend without Premier League football. However, there has been some football action around LFC during past days.

For instance, last Thursday a game was played at Anfield. Nothing less than the miniderby, between LFC reserves and Everton reserves, which carried a lot of expectation. So much so that they decided to play it at Anfield, in front of more that 2.000 people. It was a very good game. Not perfect, of course. To begin with, the result was a disappointing draw, 2-2. And there was mistakes, bad decisions,…But overall a game definitely worth watching.

Not for the first time this season, a game of the reserves, or U18, has been, in terms of pure football, way more enjoyable than many of first team's games. Take out of this assertion the ManU game, of course. And maybe 4 or 5 others. But the Youth Cup matches, particularly that 3-1 against Crystal Palace, have been outstanding. Also the 9-0 win against Southend, but even Borrell said that the really good match was that 3-1. And what a season if a 9-0 win is not the best match! Even the 3-2 defeat against ManU was a fairly well played game, frustrating as it was.

Frustrating was also last Saturday 2-4 defeat against Nott Forest. The team was without many of its best players due to international duties. Notwithstanding that, the players gave a really good account of themselves during long spells of the game. However, repeated defence mistakes ("ridiculous", as Borrell said) cost and the team their first league defeat since October. Having not been so impressive, the reserves have also offered good pieces of football, even if there has been a change of coach recently. McMahon did a good job, but he seemed to have lost ground with the rest of the Academy coaching staff, so let's hope his replacement will have good effect on the team and the development of the players.

The miniderby showed promising things, I reckon. In only his second match as reserves coach, Pep Segura displayed a solid team, with Irwin behind the strikers and Roberts and Thomas securing the midfield. In the wings, Suso and Ince were expected to provide ammunition for Saric, with the assistance of Flanagan and Robinson as full backs. As center backs, Wisdom and Mendy were protecting the goalkeeper, Hansen.

During the first half, LFC were in charge with a commanding display, but lacked the final touch. Although the intentions were clear, and they tried to play good football, they found it difficult to cause real damage to Everton defence. Even so, being 2-0 down at halftime was tough to take, and not only because the penalty missed by Roberts. Two very well taken goals by Everton, no doubt; but clearly against the run of play. The reaction after halftime was impressive. The tactic changes proved to be extremely effective. Tony Silva replaced Thomas and played on the right; Suso went on to operate behind the striker, and Irwin moved to midfield, always with an eye on supporting the attack. The basic idea of play remained the same. Ball possession, good movements, passing game, looking for the chance to get behind the defenders. But the new team had more invention, more flair, and goal chances began to appear. The game was levelled with more than 20 minutes left, and a win seemed likely.

But it wasn't to be. Partly due to some mistakes in the final touch, or the final pass, partly due to the players being tired, or some lack of composure,...the game ended 2-2. But it was surely a great experience for the players. By far, the best Suso has played at reserve level, showing some of the magic we had already seen with the U18. Very good game by Flanagan and Robinson, offering constant support from the flanks. Roberts managed the game very well, despite his penalty miss. All in all, a good football match, that will do no harm to the progress of the players.

Which should be the ultimate aim of the reserves teams, and the reserves league, but I am not convinced it is the case now in England. The U18 playing without half of the team because of their very success that has lead to the players going on international duties, or the irregularity of the calendar both for the reserves (they spent in the region of three full months without a league game last winter) and the U18 makes me wonder if this is really the best way to develop players.

At those ages a player needs, more than anything, time on the pitch, in competitive games. And they are not getting it in the current system. I guess that it is a system from a time in which reserves teams were properly that. But now almost every reserve team is really a different team, the last stage of the formative process, and they need more competitive games, and a more balanced schedule.

Furthermore, I am not sure to what extent it is appropriate for the staff to keep saying that "the important thing" is to educate the players and that "the results don't count". Don't get me wrong. It is clear that the main aim is to get players ready for the first team; but probably one mean to that end is to give importance to the results, precisely as part of that education. Otherwise, the players will not learn to compete effectively, and are bound to feel the pressure of the first team much more.

Maybe, this is one of the factors behind England national teams repeated failures in senior international competitions. After all, the clubs can simply turn to foreign players (which they do), something the national team cannot do. As a foreigner myself, I am not in the best position for fully understand all the details, but while I don't know what is the solution, I am almost certain that something needs to be changed in the organization of the youngster teams competitions.

Anyway, may the Premier League return soon (yes, even this season).

8.- Difficult to find words

Date: 5-April-2011
Previous results: WBA 3-1 LFC (Premier League); ManU U18 1-2 LFC U18; Aston Villa Reserves 3-1 LFC Reserves

What could you say about the West Bromwich match that has not been said by now? Or, for that matter, that has been said yet. (Just in case anyone has recognized the sentence: yes, it is a conscious tribute to Argentineans Les Luthiers). It is often said that if you have nothing nice to say, you should not say anything at all. I don't know to what extent you agree with that statement, but the problem in these days for us, LFC fans, is that, with that in mind, we should remain absolutely silent.

What nice things could be said about that match from LFC point of view? Well, certainly Reina played as well as he ever has played for us. Which, on the other hand, is hardly a good thing for LFC. But the sheer truth is that, had it not been for Pepe's heroics, the score would have been a lot worse. He could probably have avoided that last penalty, but he is not the one to blame, neither for that second goal nor for the whole match performance.

If I had to look on the bright side, I would direct my eyes to the Academy, of course. A win over ManU, even at U18 level, is always good news. And there was that cup defeat that needed some kind of revenge. The reserves showed some good things in their defeat against an experienced Aston Villa team (not the least the Silva goal), although it was not a good game overall.

But it is the first team which is worrying. Once again this season, both under Roy Hodgson and under Kenny Dalglish, we saw a match that confronts us with a reality that we often prefer not to face. It is very good to keep saying that the lack of funding, and the actions of former owners, prevents us from playing on a level field against ManU, Chelsea, Arsenal, Man City, (even Tottenham?).

But if any of you needed to pick a starting eleven between Carson, Reid, Olsson, Meité, Shorey, Mulumbu, Scharner, Thomas, Brunt, Cox, Odemwingie, Reina, Carragher, Skrtel, Kyrgiakos, Wilson, Leiva, Spearing, Kuyt, Meireles, Suarez and Carroll (note that I include those two injuries of Johnson and Agger), how many of the first eleven would make it to your team?

Either the answer is almost none, and in that case we need to look for an explanation for that performance, so poor that I can hardly find words to describe, or the answer is that many of them, and in that case the money for transfer fees and wages is not to blame.

The appointment of Kenny Dalglish has had a reinvigorating effect on the team, the whole club, the fans,...and we would probably not be 6th in the Premier League table had it not been for him. But he and his staff seem to struggle when they need to plan matches against the low tier teams. They were brilliant in the matches against ManU and Chelsea, but the matches against Wigan, West Ham, or the European ones, have shown a very poor team.

And not only needs to be addressed the pure football side of the performance of the team, but also the management of the matches by the players. If you are playing so poorly and, out of the blue, you find yourself ahead in the score in the second half against a team like West Brom, you don't lose the match. You shouldn't even draw the match. Simply a composed display, a professional control of the game, should have been enough to keep West Brom far from Pepe. Moreover, if you can count on a great match by your goalkeeper, then the game should be closed.

But they couldn't do that. The players weren't able to keep the ball, sometimes they seemed incapable of the most simple passes. It was very disappointing a match. I am sure Dalglish, Clarke and Lee were angry. I am sure the players were angry, too. But it is not the first time in the season that something similar happens. And apparently there are no remedies at hand.

But if that is the case, then we don't need two or three players in the summer to be competitive again. We would need not less that seven or eight. That is for Comolly and Dalglish (and/or the next manager, whoever he is) to ponder, and I very much hope that they get it right in the transfer market. But there are no excuses that LFC team cannot compete, not with ManU or Man City, but with Wigan, West Ham, or West Bromwich.

As for the rest of the season, if King Kenny can keep on handling brilliantly the big games, then Man City, Tottenham and Arsenal may be great to watch. Let's hope so, beginning next Monday.

I don't want to finish this post without biding a great "Happy birthday" to María. She is a key person in the LFC community for many of us who know her. She is the kind of person that would probably have said nothing about LFC this week, having nothing nice to say.

9.- *Regularity and brilliance*

Date: 14-April-2011
Previous results: LFC 3-0 Man City (Premier League)

After what was a magnificent display by the team, against Man City, we have been left with no option but ask the Premier League for a schedule in which LFC always face the top teams. ManU: a big win at home, a narrow defeat away (twice, as a matter of fact, including the FA Cup); Chelsea: two clear victories; Man City; one clear defeat, one clear victory; Arsenal: one unfair draw, that should have been a 10-man victory; Tottenham: an extremely unfair defeat.

Meanwhile, Blackpool made the double against us, and we have conceded defeats against West Ham, Stoke, Newcastle, Blackburn, Wolves,...not to mention Braga or, yes, Northampton. And the list is not complete, feel free to add more games. Both sets of matches, against top teams and not-so-top teams, brilliant and embarrassing, occurred under Hodgson and under Dalglish. So maybe is the players we should look at in search of an explanation. An explanation that I don't have. It is hard to think the brilliant team that totally outplayed Man City is, give or take, the same team that gave so poor a performance as the West Brom match, to name just one.

So, while these days are days of proud and joy, lets not lose sight of the fact that the team is almost impossible to understand. I guess than even Hodgson was, and Dalglish is, wondering what exactly is happening here. I for one am switching between the thought that the team is only 2/3 players away from being a genuine title contender next season, and the thought that a major revamp is needed, with some seasons before we can aim at major titles again. I guess I am not alone in this state of constant change in mood.

However, as said above, now it is the moment to rejoice in what was a great performance, especially during the first half. Energy, high tempo, pass and move, press, movement, verticality, aim at goal,...The first team was unbearable for the Man City team. Barry and Toure could hardly notice Leiva and Spearing, both defending and attacking; the location of Kuyt at any given moment was an unsolved equation for Kolarov and Milner; Carroll tormented Kompany and Lescott, who at the same time had to cope with Suarez, who always was where less expected; Meireles moved in and out, supporting the midfielders while attending the left side. All of it resulting in Hart being fortunate for only picking the ball from the net three times.

Moreover, the defenders were spot on in almost all their movements, with and without the ball. It was hard to believe that Flanagan was having his first outing with the first team, always focused, assured, and in his position. Although probably, with Carra there, almost all of us would have offered a fully focused performance. Flanagan was not got passed once, there was not even the least danger from the right side. On the other side, Aurelio, after quite a bit time out of the team, had the only troubles against Johnson, but he, with the help of his team mates, was able to cope with it and remain undamaged. Carragher was as solid as you can hope for, and I want to say that Skrtel played arguably his best match in a LFC shirt. I have criticised him quite a lot, but I have to admit that in this match he was outstanding in all he had to do.

Also encouraging was the balance between long and short balls, between going through the wings or through the middle, between the fast counterattack and the control of the ball and game. The defenders could always found Leiva or Spearing ready to get the ball and play it the way it needed to be played. Kuyt and Meireles knew when widen the field and when go inside to help. Suarez and Carroll added to the team efforts with their constant movement, not always rewarded by a pass, but fruitful in opening spaces for their team mates.

So, was it the best match any team (not only LFC) has ever (not only this season) played? No. And not even close. There were lost passes, unsuccessful dribbles, bad defensive movements, poor choices between options,…as there are in every football match. In fact, it is particularly difficult to find an undisputed MOTM. No player was at his peak (maybe with the exception of Skrtel), but all of them where at a good level. Every player has had better games before, but the overall display was impressive. In a way, there is a good symptom that the team performed so well without any particular player over his own level. All the players gave solid and good displays, but in every case within their expected level. All of that referring to the first half. The second half was slightly different. It was well played, Man City having no options to get back in the match. And a couple more goals could have followed, but the team opted, and rightly so, for remain solid, and they lowered a little bit the standard of play. Not that I am complaining. It was probably what was needed in that situation, and LFC were never in danger of losing the advantage.

The two players I would like to particularly praise are Flanagan and Spearing. Flanagan went forward much less than he usually does in the U18 team. But there was not need of that in the match. He choose carefully and, in doubt, he opted for remain in defence, which was a shrewd decision. On the other hand, while in possession he not only hardly missed a ball; he in fact almost always gave the appropriate pass, and then moved to be available to the other players, if needed. So, not spectacular, but a very good debut. There is much more to come from him, I hope.

As for Spearing, he is having a bit of a rollercoaster season, with good and poor performances. But he is a real midfielder. He knows where to go to get the ball, and what to do with the ball. Ha has in him a wide range of passes, and can dictate the play. He is the only midfielder that currently offers the team a good ball movement. He works tirelessly for the team, and I am sure that Barry and Toure are still wondering where all that energy came from. He is still growing as a player in the team, and can be a very good asset in the months and seasons ahead. Probably not an automatic first team choice in the future, but always good to have in the squad. Maybe key in the end of this season.

Rejoice finished. The team needs to start being much more regular. A good run of games, while most probably not enough for getting to 5th place, will help face the summer preparations, and the beginning of next season, more positively. And will help the technical staff to make good transfer decisions. Still, as the next match is against Arsenal, it would be fine if the players can focus in keeping their usual level against top teams. The regularity can come after that.

Justice for the 96. YNWA.

10.- Magical thinking, logical thinking

Date: 18-April-2011
Previous results: Arsenal 1-1 LFC (Premier League)

The final stages of Arsenal match appealed to that magical thinking we all have inside us, didn't it? It is tempting to think in some magical fate to explain how on Earth a team stripped of their more recognisable players can draw a match they are losing well inside injury time.

From the middle of the second half on, LFC were without their complete first-choice defence (Johnson, Carragher, Agger, Aurelio), their captain and arguably best player (Gerrard), and their most expensive signing (Carroll). They were playing against a top team, a title contender, in an away match. And still they managed to go through with the score at 0-0, and relatively undamaged in terms of clear chances, Reina mostly uncalled to act.

Surely they were buried after that last minute penalty scored by Van Persie. Surely? Well, think again. Out of the blue, LFC players kept the faith in themselves, threw everything on Arsenal goal and, well, the (almost) unthinkable happened. In the end, 1-1, and LFC still unbeatable by the top teams in this second half of the season.

Many of LFC fans have surely thought that Dalglish was key to the late developments, and that it would have never happened under Hodgson. That the close connection between the "Holy Trinity" Shankly once spoke about (the players, the manager and the supporters) is responsible for that nearly miraculous recovery.

Well, to this point the magical thinking. And I would really agree that there are good points there, difficult to contradict. But, as rewarding and pleasant as those magical and irrational moments are (and they surely are, they are the reason many of us are football supporters), in order to improve we have also to apply logical thinking to the matches.

Because magical moments should be the icing on the cake, and not the bread and butter for a top tier football club. It is great to do an Istambul in a Champions League final, but to get there you need to consistently beat a number of clubs in a more regular manner.

So, what were the good things LFC did until the 95th minute? And what were the bad things? We all are proud of that final moment; and deservedly so. But should we be as proud of the rest of the match?

Almost any pundit will have their own answer to those questions, and I don't pretend to have a definite answer. In short, my easy answer would be that there were many encouraging things in the match, but also some shortcomings.

Probably LFC should be able to be more dominant during the matches. Against Arsenal, and unlike the match against Man City, for long periods of time our team was unable to keep and pass the ball, to get to the Arsenal box with enough number of players to really cause troubles, to dictate the game. We were left to simply defend-and-lose-the-ball too many times, particularly in the second half.

Of course, in front there was one of the better teams in Europe; but, precisely in order to reach that level, the team must improve on that field. The centre backs struggled to play the ball, the full backs almost never got to the opposite half, the centre midfielders found it difficult to hold on to the ball, the wing midfielders got isolated from the core of play, unable to effectively help their team mates, and the forwards were outnumbered by Arsenal defenders.

On the other hand, the defensive side of the team was excellent. As said before, Reina needed to make only one really difficult save, and Arsenal was unable to create real danger. The centre backs, even with Skrtel and Kyrgiakos on the pitch, gave a solid display; Flanagan and Robinson, in their second first team outing, were firm and stopped their opponents, while not easily giving the ball away. Spearing and Leiva were brilliant in deactivating the Arsenal play; only when Fabregas and Nasri connected could they cause some problems; Kuyt and Meireles prevented Eboue and Clichy from helping their attack forces, and Suarez and Carroll pressed and troubled the ball circulation.

Well, that is obviously a brief and overall assessment. There were times in which LFC went forward, created chances, and threatened the Arsenal defence. It was not by any means and all-and-only defensive game. But, as the match was approaching its end, LFC were more and more reduced to their own half.

Still, judging by the first 95 minutes, I would give the team performance a fairly high note; not excellent, but composed and solid. Good if taken as a step forward, as a stage in the road; not good enough as the definite product from a LFC side.

And then the final madness came. After conceding the goal, it was a moment for lamenting the bad luck, licking the wounds, speaking of the proud of a good display and the promising youngsters, and getting back home. I am sure those were more or less the thoughts of all but eleven men. Luckily enough, there were those eleven men who counted. And they indeed made themselves count. What resilience.

So, magical thinking and logical thinking. Let us enjoy the last moments, the exhilaration, the bravery, the never-say-die attitude, the sheer pride of being part of this football club. But also analysis, feet on the ground, and keeping the expectation level for a club the size of LFC. Expectation level that should be closer to the Man City match than to the Arsenal match. And standard of play that should be translated into the matches against not so glamorous teams, beginning with Birmingham.

11.- Goals for fun

Date: 3-May-2011
Previous results: LFC 5-0 Birmingham (Premier League); LFC 3-0 Newcastle (Premier League)

Fifth spot in the table, eight goals scored, two clean sheets, two wins,...The things could have hardly gone better for LFC in the last two league games from the statistical point of view. However, it is in the good times in which a cool head and clear thinking and analysis are more needed, and I guess that there are plenty of issues to assess, as for the level of play of the team.

Firstly, I need to admit that I didn't watch the whole 5-0 against Birmingham, so what I am going to write is mostly based in the 3-0 against Newcastle and the highlights of the Birmingham game. And I don't think that the Newcastle game was a good one. Clearly, the final score was as good as one may have expected, no doubt about that. But the standard of play was way below that.

The team never really fought for the ball, nor tried to take the game to the Newcastle half. And I am under the impression that something similar happened during Birmingham game. LFC simply waited in its own half for Newcastle to lose the ball, and relied on Suarez and Kuyt to win long balls and mount the attack from there.

I don't know about the rest of the fans, but that is not really the type of football I want to see from LFC, even less in Anfield in front of a team that had lost the match before the initial whistle. To clarify: the matches against Man U, and Man City were great displays of football. Sometimes you need to take a step back to protect yourself and damage the opposition. I don't think that was the case last Sunday.

LFC looked more for punishing Newcastle mistakes than for creating their own luck. And that is hardly a path to greatness. Some years ago, a cycling pundit said that there were three riders that could win that particular race on merit, and ten others that could, given the appropriate situation, take advantage of specific circumstances to eventually win. In my view, LFC should be a team that works its own circumstances, not merely a team that banks on other teams' mistakes.

And that was not the team I saw against Newcastle. The main game plan seemed to be waiting for the mistakes of Newcastle and use the quality of LFC players to score, while keeping the players well placed at any given moment to prevent Newcastle from even approaching Reina. That may sound good and clever. That may be good and clever. But it is not a way to winning league titles.

On a more specific note regarding the Newcastle match, I hope the match serves as a wake up call to Flanagan. Very promising player, having had a fairy tale season so far: dominant for the U18, accomplished for the reserves, and a very good starting in the first team. But he had many problems last Sunday, he tasted what it is like playing at top level. I do think that he has all the potential in him to fulfil all the expectations put in him, but he is not the finished article by now, and he needs to work hard.

Skrtel and Carragher did OK; Johnson was fine, but I was left a little bit disappointed by his lack of attacking play in the second half, back to where he belongs, the right side of the pitch. Lucas and Spearing where great defensively; they managed to handle almost all of the Newcastle attack. But they did not do so well on the attacking side. They struggled to receive the ball from the defences and carry it to the forwards, and failed to really dictate the match.

Well, to this point I am being harsh with the team, after two, 5-0 and 3-0, wins, I am afraid. There were also positives, of course. Let's turn to them. The four attacking-minded players (Kuyt, Maxi, Meireles and Suarez) did a great job in both matches, constantly interchanging his positions, with great mobility, making themselves unreadable for the opposition defence.

On top of that, they were clinical, putting in the net almost every suitable ball that they could get. Against Newcastle, and I think against Birmingham, too, there were not many clear chances, but the converting rate was phenomenal. Probably Meireles is a little bit out of rhythm now. He was outstanding in January, but he seems to have lost his reading of the matches, his pace. Maxi looks on fire now, with little participation on the play, but always in place to get the goal needed.

And Kuyt and Suarez are unstoppable. They cannot stay calm, always running, opening spaces, offering passes to their team-mates, troubling the full backs as much as the centre backs. And, of course, getting and creating the goals (the finishing of Kuyt in the Birmingham goal was terrific).

And, also on the plus side, it is worth having in mind that the ability to produce, to get goals, to keep clean sheets, to win matches, while not playing at full potential, is essential in the process towards winning leagues. So, if the case is that of a poorly played match from which a win is dragged, that is great news. But the ambition to play much better should be within the team.

Hopefully next Monday we will be talking about three victories, three clean sheets, eleven or twelve goals,...and a better performance.

12.- The definite proof

Date: 13-May-2011
Previous results: Fulham 2-5 LFC (Premier League)

One thing maybe every football supporter have asked himself at least once (surely I have) is about the decision making process inside a football club. How an ordinary man reaches the conclusion that a certain player is worth 50 mill.? Or 35 mill.? Or that certain other (or the same) player should be deemed surplus to requirements and an offer for him accepted?

That question arises this week in the context of the announcement of Kenny Dalglish being appointed manager of the club, in a three year contract. Why now? Why not a month ago? Why not in a couple of weeks? What is the main factor besides that decision? A decision that has two parts: deciding to offer the post to him, and deciding to make it public precisely now.

Probably when back in January the post was offered on a temporary basis the idea was. "Well, this season cannot get worse; lets have a look if Dalglish has got what it takes to manage a team in these times, and at the end of the season we may, or may not, make his appointment permanent". Fair enough, not a bad idea. But, after that, how is it judged if he "has got what it takes". Is it a certain number of points? Is it the feel good factor in Melwood? Is it the tactics in the games? Is it the impression Dalglish conveys when talking to the directors? Is it the ability to recruit the players and coaches needed?

Luckily for the main executives, Kenny Dalglish seems to have nailed it in all those fields. So there was possibly little doubt about him being the right man in the right moment. (Let's not forget, however, that similar conclusion can be drawn from the work of Hodgson in West Bromwich; but that is a different story). But keep in mind that the task ahead is different from that that has been brilliantly accomplished. It is one thing to lift the spirits of a very demoralised squad, and steer them through the rest of what could have been a very, very disappointing season, which Dalglish have excelled at; and another different thing to turn the squad in one really capable of challenging for mayor honours.

So the board of directors had to decide whether or not to hand the post to Dalglish; and also had to decide when take that step; and then, when should it be make public. And that process is really the one I would like very much to know about. The timing of the operation seems to point at the Fulham game as the turning point, the definite proof. It is clearly naïve to make that assumption, but it is tempting, isn't it?

Winning an away match against a top opponent: checked (Chelsea)
Consistently winning home matches: checked.
Winning a home match against a top opponent: checked (ManU)
Absolute demolition of a top four team: checked (Man City)
Away victories: checked (Sunderland)
Resilience in a difficult environment: checked (Arsenal)

Mmmmm...What is missing?... Scoring for fun in away games!: checked (Fulham)

It was a great match. Far from perfect, but for the first time in a while LFC appeared to get to the pitch ready to go for the match from the beginning. And when things went our way, the team kept pushing, kept playing. Or trying to play, at least. There were several moments during the match in which LFC lost their pace, lost the control of the match, and even suffered. This team is still unfinished business, but it was reassuring to see them sticking together, showing commitment between them, and a sheer determination not to let the match go, irrespective of the difficulties. The improvements needed are there for anyone to see, but the spirit and ambition were also for anyone to see.

Most probably, the decision to make Dalglish the permanent was made well before Fulham game, but it seemed to complete the circle. The team looks now stronger than at any other time in the season, and probably the directors wanted to express their support before the deciding game against Tottenham. I am not sure if that has been the right moment, only next Sunday will bring the answer.

Even if the team finishes 6th it will have been a great string of matches since Dalglish took the reins. Still, it will be better not to lose the perspective. There also have been bad moments, and disappointments those last months. And the level of play has not always been LFC standard. But the overall judgement must be clearly positive. The challenge now is to improve and transfer the good aspects into the new season, while showing a lasting title level. We have seen many very good half-seasons in last years. We need a very good whole season.

How far the squad is from being a title winning squad is hard to say. I would think that in the summer of 2002, or 2009, things looked brighter. But both of them ended in failure, so who knows?

Let's hope that decision making process regarding the appointment of Dalglish prove to be hugely successful in seasons ahead, and the team can bring back glory days.

13.- Can such a thing as a "blessing in disguise" really exist?

Date: 20-May-2011
Previous results: LFC 0-2 Tottenham (Premier League)

English not being my first language, one thing I usually notice is the "idioms" used in interviews, news, articles,...Now and then, I find one of those idioms particularly catchy, which is precisely the case with that "blessing in disguise". I have always seen it used related to football matters, probably because we football fans tend to be "hope prone", and ready to find the brilliant aspects of even the most evident defeats. Although sometimes we must admit that the "disguise" is very, very good, and the blessing hard to find.

Such expression has been widely used in last months regarding the possibility (weeks ago almost the certainty) of LFC not reaching qualification for international competitions next season. So, it was argued, next season LFC would be able to fully focus on domestic issues, would avoid long trips, and would be more likely to success. Which is all very well, but forgets the very aim of every football team: being at every moment as successful as possible, getting in the table as high as possible, reaching in the cup competitions the later stages as possible. Moreover, lets not skip the fact that a great deal of LFC legend is based on European competitions, beginning, on the managerial side, with Shankly and finishing (up to date) with Benitez, with the notable exception in between of...Kenny Dalglish. While very few (if any) would dispute that the Dalglish team in the 80's would achieved great European success had it not been for the banning, I couldn't imagine Dalglish willingly letting pass the chance of winning a European trophy.

And that chance has been hardly damaged by last weekend match against Tottenham. Hopefully the team can make amends in the last match of the season, and I wouldn't completely rule out the possibility, given the difficulties Tottenham are experiencing of late, and the situation of Birmingham wanting to avoid relegation but, as of now, it seems unlikely we are going to see European football at Anfield next season. As I have argued before, I don't think that is, in any case, a blessing. Europe League has served LFC well during the 2010/2011 season, it has provided the youngsters with invaluable first team experience, it gave a sense of success when league form was really poor. And it was nothing but a shame that LFC were knocked out so early, and couldn't go on.

Still, what about the Tottenham match? With all the disappointment around the outcome of the match, I do think there were positives to take from it, both short and long term. That match may be a blessing in a very sophisticated disguise. The players entered the field with their minds in other place, or at least it seemed so. Probably all the euphoria in the previous week (reaching the 5th spot, the appointment of Dalglish, the fans almost taken a victory for granted,...) cost in a way. Not deliberately, of course, but one could get the impression that the players were not fully focused. That was obviously negative; still, I think it was positive, and testimony to the player's commitment and confidence that they were able to turn things and get into the match, at around 20/25 minutes. It is not easy to do that.

Usually, when you are out of focus, you have to wait until halftime to revert the situation, but the players achieved that during the first half. That was a positive, in my view.

Not that they played to their standards, but at least they took the game to Tottenham, even if lacking clear goal chances, and real damage to Tottenham defence. The second half was really more of the same. Certain sense of LFC dictating the game, playing in opposition field, but without creating first quality football. The penalty decision, harsh as they come, virtually put an end to the match, result wise. As for individual performances, it is noticeable how Suarez started the game absolutely out of himself. Diving, confronting rivals, disagreeing with the referee and even team mates, losing balls,...But, credit to him, he was able to somehow mirror the team in eventually getting into the match and causing some, even if minor, problems to the Tottenham defence. Carroll, on the other side, had a very poor match. Blame it on the injuries, if you want, but he seemed to be playing a different match from the other players. I hope the summer and preseason can turn him into a player more valuable to the team.

Not very much else stood out. Reina had hardly anything to do; the defenders were OK, with both full backs adding to the attack more than in other matches; Spearing and Lucas managed the ball well, but failed to do real harm; Kuyt and Maxi had an indifferent match, after some brilliant games of late. Bench players didn't change things, and I wonder why Cole didn't play before; or, for that matter, why was sent to the pitch at such a late stage.

So, the reaction of the players midway the first half is a positive sign for the future. And another positive, what might be the real "blessing" from the match, is probably to have confronted LFC with their own reality. This squad is still way short of a proper title contender one. One could have been tempted, by previous results, to think that a couple of minor adjustments could do for next season, but Tottenham game display states clearly that some major improvements are needed if the team is to at least mount a credible challenge for the title next year, in which a top four spot will be an absolute must.

Surely the club personnel are working hard on the next season squad, even more after the confirmation of Dalglish appointment. Hopefully they are right in their decisions during what seems to be a defining transfer window for LFC. Summers of 2002 and 2009 were failed transfer windows, and the club couldn't capitalise on good seasons; summer of 2010, on the other hand, was fairly OK in roughly keeping the team at their previous level; the addition of Meireles have proved to be useful to the team. Summer of 2011, however, needs to be more decisive, and keeping the level is not an option; the level of the squad needs to be clearly raised. Even if, after all, LFC reach the 5th spot (which, at least by me, would be warmly welcome).

If Tottenham match has served as a wake up call regarding the needs of the team and squad (I don't think Dalglish, Clarke and Comolli needed that call, but many fans, and maybe directors, did), I will be happy to call it a blessing in disguise and add it to my English repertoire.

SEASON 2011/2012

14.- Football again

Date: 16-July-2011
Previous results: Pre-season, Guandong 3-4 LFC; Malaysia XI 3-6 LFC

After roughly two months waiting for it, football season is again with us. Well, not proper season, but at least friendly matches, which are thoroughly scrutinised (in fact, very often even more carefully scrutinised than official matches; we the fans have been without material to think and talk about for much time, and want to reach "definitive" conclusions of the state of the team ahead of the proper season).

I had the chance to watch the second half of last Wednesday match, and the full game of today. More or less like any other fan I feel in the position to assess the full next season after that. I have reasons for optimism, for pessimism, for scepticism, for enthusiasm…

Equally like almost any other fan I remind myself of the real circumstances. The players are only beginning to play, the matches are unofficial, there is almost a complete team missing. I know, by years of experience, that almost nothing can be known by now, the opposition have not been anywhere close the real teams we are going to face during the season,…

But I want to discuss football, I want to think about it, I want to make predictions, I want to share views with fellow fans,…So, briefly, here we come.

Judging only the Saturday match, here is how I have seen the players, and the team. In order to avoid excessive analysis, I have opted to divide the players in only three groups: those who performed more or less as expected; those who performed better; and those who performed worse.

As I see it, players that gave an only standard version of themselves include: Jones, Carragher, Robinson, Spearing, Coady, Carroll, Gulacsi, Kelly, Kyrgiakos, Poulsen, Shelvey, and Kuyt. Some of them played a little bit better than others but, overall, I would say that they offered an indifferent display, the one you can expect at this time of the season.

Players that performed poorly would be: Hansen, Flanagan, Agger, Wilson, Meireles, Maxi. Maybe this last one should be explained, but I really think that Maxi didn't add anything to the team...apart from poaching two goals. We can argue endlessly about that being enough, but especially in pre-season I want to see players contributing to the team.

And players that gave a particularly satisfactory impression were: Adam, Cole, Insua, Aquilani, Ngog. Adam looked very lively in recovering the ball in midfield, and put a couple of good crosses in the box; Cole got involved in the play, associated with any other player, tried some dangerous passes into the box, and showed some quality; Insua got forward time and again, made good crosses, added to the attacking side; Ngog moved well, looked for the ball, finished well.

And the absolute man of the match, head and shoulders above the rest, Aquilani. He missed some passes, and made mistakes, but always kept the ball moving, tried to help his team mates, found the better spaces where to do damage to the opposition. And even tried, and almost got, an Alonso-esque goal from midfield. It will be a shame when he finally, as it seems almost sure, leave the team.

As for the team as a whole, there were encouraging signs of wanting to keep the ball, trying to find spaces through the possession and movement, dictating the course of the game. But, obviously, before we get too carried away we need to think on the size of the opposition. More worrying was the lack of intensity in defence. Precisely because the rivals being so poor, conceding three goals is not a good outcome. Lets hope that will be sorted out in training sessions.

All that said, nothing of this is of much significance. More than half the presumed starting team during the season was not even in the same continent; some players will leave, other will come. But, after so much time without LFC matches, I cannot help trying to draw and share with you kopites some conclusions, irrelevant as they may be.

15.- Foundations for success

Date: 13-October-2011
Previous results: ; Hull 3-0 LFC (Pre-season Friendly); Galatasaray 3-0 LFC (Pre-season Friendly); Valerenga 3-3 LFC (Pre-season Friendly); LFC 2-0 Valencia (Pre-season Friendly); LFC 1-1 Sunderland (Premier League); Arsenal 0-2 LFC (Premier League); Exeter 1-3 LFC (Carling Cup); LFC 3-1 Bolton (Premier League); Stoke 1-0 LFC (Premier League); Tottenham 4-0 LFC (Premier League); Brighton 1-2 LFC (Carling Cup); LFC 2-1 Wolves (Premier League); Everton 0-2 LFC (Premier League)

There is a well known Spanish football pundit that keeps on saying, time and again, that for a football team to really succeed, on a long-term basis, it is of paramount importance to have a strong block between the goalkeeper and the central defenders. I really think that this is one of the problems that have had LFC struggling during last seasons.

Not that there is a particular problem with the goalkeeper. Reina has been a little bit inconsistent at some times, but overall he is a very good goalkeeper. However, the central defenders are a different story.

Many of us, having experienced it first hand or listened to others, know how Shankly built his first great team almost literally on the shoulders of the giant Ron Yeats; not to mention, during the following years, the likes of Hughes, Thompson, Lawrenson, Hansen, Hysen,…Every LFC fan could mention without difficulties not only great forwards and midfielders, but also outstanding central defenders.

That is also true for the last title winning LFC teams, from the Henchoz/Hyypia partnership that flourished under Houllier (one interesting case of two players that were even better as a pair than individually), leading the team to the 2001 treble, and the 2002 2nd position in the League, until Carragher/Hyypia leading the team to Estambul, and another 2nd position in the League.

Of course, both Houllier and Benitez achieved other titles and successes, always relying in great central defenders, which almost never got injured or sent off. Around them, the team would gather and grow, becoming a formidable force. One of the great, and often unsung, merits of Benitez was to forecast the end of the Henchoz/Hyypia partnership and set a new pair, Carragher/Hyypia, that in time would prove to be even better.

That is something LFC have been missing in last seasons. After Hyypia started to lose effectiveness, Carragher managed to almost single-handedly keep the solidity at the back for a while. And, had Agger not been so unlucky with the injuries (or so injury-prone, depending on the point of view), the problem would have been postponed. But with Agger only able to play in the region of 25/30 matches a season, in the best scenario, LFC is currently in huge troubles.

Carragher, loyal servant and true legend as he is, has his best playing years well behind him, and should only be asked to help, and fill in when needed, but not to be the key player he continues to be.

Agger is potentially a top-class central defender, a really great player with the ability both to defend and to go forward, to intercept the opposition play and to create the LFC attack, equally comfortable in the ground and in the air. His only problem is the amount of time he spends in the sidelines. We are always hoping for a season in which he can play more than 40 matches, which could make the world of a difference in an LFC season.

Skrtel is not a player the size of LFC. He might be a useful cover for central defenders in not very challenging matches. And, of course, never as a right back; although this right back position is not his fault, and he performs as he could. But even as a central defender he is not top-team material. He may be successful in, say, Sunderland, Bolton, WBA,...but not in a team aiming at the top of the table.

Coates is the last addition. I have not seen enough of him to make a judgement. Still, it seems that he has been brought with a view on the future, more than on the present. If that is the case, he is not helpful to solve the current problem. Moreover, if he is not better than Skrtel as of now, I seriously doubt he will be really great in the future. Still, it is early days to judge him.

Finally, Wilson has given little ground for hope in the few matches he has played as a centre back. And he is not in the picture for the technical staff in this moment.

Other options in the near future? Well, many of us are hoping to see Martin Kelly play as a centre back. I think he may be a great asset if given the time and confidence. But I honestly don't know. Wisdom looks a promising player, but he is probably at least 2/3 years away from being a first team regular.

One friend of mine has an interesting theory: according to him, there are few really great central defenders that are extremely good by themselves. And other good ones that can perform very well if paired with them, but not if paired with other centre back. Today's versions of Carragher, Skrtel, and Coates lay at best in that second category, with Agger being in the first one. But it means that, with Agger out of the team, LFC have not reliable pair of central defenders.

When compared with the string of central defenders in the really great squads (Ferdinand-Vidic-Evans-Jones-Smalling, Lescott-Kompany-Touré, Terry-Luiz-Ivanovic-Alex, Piqué-Puyol-Mascherano-Abidal, Pepe-Carvalho-Albiol-Varane, amongst other cases), LFC are obviously struggling. And that accounts in great part for the hard times in the Premier League in recent times.

LFC are more than able of winning any given game. Hopefully they will prove it as soon as next Saturday. But they are extremely unlikely to win the Premier, or even any major title; at least until a couple of great centre backs are bought (or one bought and Coates proving to be one of them). Gerrard-Kuyt-Suarez-Bellamy-Carroll can be a torture for any defence; but almost any forward in the Premier League can be a real headache for LFC defenders.

Hopefully the coming transfer windows will see this issue adequately addressed. And I can stop listening to that pundit saying that LFC really need new solid foundations to become again a real force in the game.

Ah! And obviously let's hope for a victory against ManU, after a week without Premier League.

16.- The many halves in a glass

Date: 20-October-2011
Previous results: LFC 1-1 ManUnited (Premier League); Rangers 1-0 LFC (Friendly)

The Saturday match against ManU left me with so mixed feelings that I am honestly unable, after four days, to decide if I am more optimistic or more pessimistic than before the game. I don't know if the glass is half-empty, half-full, half-half, or what.

On the one hand, LFC were clearly the better team over the 90 minutes. The only team that deserved to win the match, the only team that played to win, attacked the rivals, and made a bold statement of intent. On the other hand, let's face it: Ferguson played a very poor team, by their standards, with nearly half his best team on the bench.

So, what should we look at? That LFC were better, or that they were incapable of winning against a well below-par ManU team?

Surely it was good to see an LFC team that went without hesitation for the match, that aimed at dictate the game, especially during the second half. At the same time, the truth is that LFC clearly struggled to impose their play against not so great a midfield. It didn't seem to be a clear game-plan to go. Probably the ManU starting eleven was so surprising for the players and technical staff that the players got a bit lost at times.

After a very promising first 10/15 minutes, LFC started to suffer and to get frustrated at every attempt. In what was a worrying fact, ManU were easily able to completely prevent the LFC defenders from properly start the play. Time and again, just three players (Park, Young and Welbeck) managed to stop six: the LFC back four plus the two central midfielders; for long minutes, it was impossible for Gerrard, Downing, Kuyt and Suarez to get into play, thus making it impossible for LFC to play to its strengths.

And playing to one's strengths in one of the secrets (not so secret, of course) of a successful team. Identifying one's strengths and opposition's weaknesses, and making them count, while avoiding and hiding one's weaknesses and opposition's strengths. LFC seemed incapable to do so in the first half. On the other hand (half-full glass), in the second half that was at least partially amended. And the game turned into LFC way.

That notwithstanding, there remained a sense that the players were not fully comfortable with the way they were playing. Apparently, the idea might have been to encourage constant interchange of positions between Gerrard, Kuyt, Downing and, to a lesser extent, Suarez or Adam. But it didn't work well, I think. The distribution of the players on the pitch was not the best, with areas overpopulated and others empty, with players stumping into each other while other parts of the pitch remained empty, LFC wise. Sometimes the wings were too detached from the central players, allowing ManU midfielders to either recover the ball from LFC feet or organise their own attack; sometimes, the whole team were too much on one side of the pitch;

sometimes the hole was in front of the midfielders, sometime behind them.

Again, something that improved after halftime, but probably there is more work on that in the training pitch needed. If the players can get it to properly work, that mobility can be a good strategy, a good way to play to LFC's strengths, given the versatility of those players. We will see how it develops in the coming weeks and matches.

Other unbalance of the team that was seen, and suffered, on Saturday, is one between the defensive and the attacking sides of the team. While the LFC attacking force can be a headache for every defence in the League, the defensive force doesn't usually convey a strong sensation. I don't know to what extent that feeling is spread within LFC fans: when I see LFC matches, I am never assured of not receiving a goal. And an opposition goal looks often easier and likelier to come. Some times it doesn't arrive, obviously, but for example I for one was not very calmed during that second half against Wolves. It seems as if an advantage of at least two goals will be needed for the team to be confident. Every player is more pressed with that fear, which often becomes some of a self-fulfilled prophecy.

One very positive note of the match was the performance by Henderson. He completely changed the game when entered the field. And changed it for the benefit of LFC. The team looked much more balanced, assured in possession, and dangerous in attack. In fact, there were probably more clear goal chances after the 1-1, with Henderson on the pitch, than before. The lad looked to be almost elsewhere, and his movements were unreadable for ManU defenders. I admit I was not a big fan of him before the match, but I am now more optimistic regarding his addition to the team. Hopefully he will build on that match and find his way to help the team improve.

Not to dismiss, of course, the great boost of the come back of Gerrard, who looked very close to his best, covering almost every inch of the pitch and going to the places of the pitch where he was most needed.

And, last but not the least, the relief of seeing an LFC team taking the match to ManU. Not trying just to capitalise on opposition mistakes, but trying to make things happen by own merit, particularly in the second half.

To sum up, both positives and negatives, reasons for optimism and pessimism. Are we aiming at first, at third or at seventh? Is winning one trophy a realistic expectation for this season? I hope this match was going to clarify, but in fact, for me, it was inconclusive. I am not any the wiser regarding the real size of the team.

So I have yet to decide if the glass is half-full, half-empty, or what. Can a glass be half-half full, half-half empty? How many halves are there in a glass?

17.- Defining moments

Date: 9-November-2011
Previous results: LFC 1-1 Norwich (Premier League); Stoke 1-2 LFC (Carling Cup); WBA 0-2 LFC (Premier League); LFC 0-0 Swansea (Premier League)

After what has been an eventful summer transfer window for LFC, it was inevitable to have an intriguing few starting weeks and matches. Would the new players settle in quickly? Would they prove to be what the squad needed? Would have the managerial staff put the team on the right track after two disappointing seasons? Would the squad really experience an improvement? Were LFC going places after all?

All sorts of questions that only actual matches could start to answer. Looking at the match schedule, the league game against ManU seemed a good point after which a first, provisional, balance could have be done. In that sense, last matches have been quite an anticlimax for LFC supporters. At least they have been for me. After a mixed start to the season, with promising signs and worrying performances, ManU match looked in fact as a suitable first defining point. Either LFC would prove themselves way below ManU, in which case we were going to face another frustrating season, or LFC would perform at least at ManU level, in which case we would know that the team could aspire to better things.

The answer…inconclusive. That was what I wrote at the time, after the match. So I needed to look for another defining point, and the international break, after an additional string of matches against low-tier teams, was as good a candidate as any other. I must admit that the answer is not inconclusive, much as I want it to have been. I feel now more pessimistic that after the ManU match.

Should I really be? Do I have reasons for that pessimism? After all, there have been no defeats in those games; two home draws (Norwich and Swansea), two away wins (Stoke and WBA). Results wise it could be argued that it has not been a terrible spell. As for the performance, there have been both positives and negatives. Unfortunately, I think the negatives bear more weight.

One of the stand-out positives is the defensive performance of the team. In those four games, two goals conceded, and two clean sheets running. After coming back to the team, Johnson looks less expansive on the attack, but pretty solid in defence. And solidity is precisely the best we can expect from Skrtel, who is providing it as of now. I stick to my old idea that he is not a top-class player, but he is fulfilling his duties fairly well. Agger is little by little getting back to his best; and he is really a great centre back, so if he can stay injury free, and close to his best level, he is going to be key to LFC season, as he has been in last matches. Jose Enrique is proving to be a great signing, adding a new dimension to a much needed left back position, although his defending is lacking a bit of consistency. As a result of the performances of the defenders, Reina is hardly being tested at all.

Obviously, defending is a task not only for the defenders, but for the whole team, and Lucas is performing well on that front. I would say that other positive is the ability of the team to create chances almost out of nothing. Jose Enrique and Suarez are the main characters in that. Their movements, their runs, their passes,...allow for an almost permanent hope that something is going to happen if the ball goes to them. Along with the odd appearances by Adam or Downing, and the set pieces with Kuyt and Carroll in the box, LFC can always be a threat to the opposition.

So, if the positives are a solid defence, and a dangerous attack, which can be the negatives?

To start with, it has to do with the general sense during the matches, the feeling that LFC is not usually dictating the play, that football is played in turn in both halves, that the following goal can go either way. That is not a good sensation for a team aiming at titles, at the top of the table.

On the defensive side of the play, there are two faces on it. On the one hand, the aim is to avoid an opposition goal. That is a task in which, as said above, the team is succeeding, even excelling. On the other hand, the aim is to take the football away from the opposite team and regain possession. In that aspect, the performances are much poorer. LFC players don't get near the rivals; don't really search for a quick recovery of the ball. I find it particularly frustrating in the midfield. Adam, Henderson, Downing, either cannot, either don't know how, recover the ball on midfield, although Suarez certainly does his bit. Opposition teams tend to look very comfortable on the ball until they are close to LFC box.

On the attacking side, the team seems lost without the intervention of Suarez. Suarez carries the ball into the box, Suarez gets the fouls, Suarez shots at goal, Suarez gives the last, and elusive, pass. There are no alternative ways to threaten the other teams, other than the crosses by Jose Enrique. Adam can make very good passes, can shoot from distance, but apparently, up to this moment, cannot step up and really dictate the play. LFC need a much steadier involvement from him (or other player; I honestly don't know if Henderson can fill that part) in organising the attack.

Those problems in both the attacking and the defensive side might have to do with the excessive distance between the players on the pitch. Thus, there is much space to defend ant to try regaining the ball, and the passes need to be longer, and more difficult, than appropriate in attack. The team needs to be more compact, both attacking and defending. But confidence is key to that; confidence that defenders can defend up in the pitch because their team-mates are going to keep the ball, and help them to recover if necessary. Confidence that midfielders can go and search the rivals because the defenders are going to be right behind them. Overall, confidence that the collective movement of the whole team is going to work well.

That kind of confidence can, of course, be built little by little on training ground, so the team can improve on that during the season. In all truth, it can take several months and even years for a team to fulfil that type of play. Why are then the negatives heavier than the positives for me as of now? The main reason is that I cannot see improvement in the team over the last weeks. They seem stagnated with little or none signs of going forward.

So I need to look at the following defining moment. Coming matches are very tough, so I will keep a close eye on the performances more than on the scores, though I will be as happy as the next guy if results come LFC way. But my next verdict may need to wait until shortly before Christmas. Let's see where we are then.

18.- Youth of today

Date: 17-November-2011
Previous results: Sporting Portugal U19 5-1 LFC U19
(NextGen Series)

Scottish author and singer Amy MacDonald has a song called "Youth of today", which I recalled yesterday as I was watching the NextGen Series match between LFC and Sporting Lisbon U19 teams. Mind you, I only recalled the title of the song, which I thought was a fitting phrase for Borrell's team. They are the youth of LFC as of today.

And that match was really a cold bath of realism. Brutal bath, at times. As Borrell himself said after the match, the gap between the teams was "massive". Which, in a way, is good. I mean, it is good for the players to confront themselves with the very best, to experience first hand what is the level expected from them, what they should aim at.

Yesterday, LFC players really struggled to keep the pace of the game as played by Sporting. Not that they were totally outclassed. During certain spells in the game LFC were able to keep and pass the ball, even to create some chances. But, overall, they were unable to stand the pass and move from Sporting during the length of the game. Very often one was under the impression that Sporting were playing with more players than LFC, reflecting the fact that, as a team, they knew better how to perform.

Borrell's team was almost in its entirety his own last year's very successful and promising U18 team. But, as in last august when both teams played at Anfield, they found that "This is the life" (yes, another Amy MacDonald song). That is the life in football if they really want to achieve first class success, as we all expect from an LFC team.

Not that they should be in anyway embarrassed. Some of the players gave a very good account of themselves. Some were only a little bit inconsistent. And some were simply worse than their opponents, but there is no shame in that, as long as you give your all, as they all did.

The goalkeeper, Belford, had in fact not very much work, weird as it may sound after receiving five goals. But he looked assured and composed in almost every ball put in the box. To what extent it is enough for a goalkeeper to be right in "almost" every ball is another matter.

As for the defenders, McGiveron was the most solid between them, but they all struggled to decipher the movements and passes of Sporting forwards. Sama and Wisdom did badly in the very decisive third and fourth goals, in which they allowed two too comfortable (though difficult, especially in the third) shoots at goal from inside the box after some poor defending in the left side. Brad Smith was somewhere in between, not as solid as McGiveron but making not clear mistakes either.

In midfield, Coady had probably one of the most frustrating games in his career. Being accustomed to rule and dictate the matches, he found it very difficult to cope with the speed of the game, the pace and quality of the passes and movements of Sporting midfielders. Hopefully this game can help him to take his game to the next level. Similar thoughts go for Roddan.

Attacking midfielders went through a very difficult game. Sterling and Adorjan were particularly unfortunate. It needs to be acknowledged that Sterling did superbly in the LFC goal, with a great run and a great cross. Still, they both need to learn more about reading matches, to know where, when and how the team needs them, whether it is on the attack or on the defence, on the flank or on the centre, helping the midfielders, or the full backs, or causing damage and troubles for the opposition. Well, at the end that is what all these matches are about, to help players to build up their game and become better footballers.

Morgan showed a handful of glimpses of his quality, with some passes and movements that reveal a very promising forward, but he was ultimately unable to really complete a good game, always behind the defenders and struggling to get some space. Ngoo was really LFC man of the match, with some extremely skilful actions. He made it very difficult for the defenders to cope with his pace and ability, and caused many problems. As is often the case in the domestic matches, it is at times frustrating to feel that he is not getting all the advantage from his conditions; but, again, matches like this will do him a lot of good.

As for the substitutes, Silva and McLaughlin were not very relevant. But very good news can be dragged from Suso's performances. He was unfulfilling this season all the expectations raised last year. But yesterday he really shone. Not exactly an unforgettable performance, but he looked very comfortable with and without the ball in what was an extremely difficult game. Hopefully he will build on that and grow from here.

Questions raised go, however, further than the match itself, and the performances by the players. The club needs to really ask why there is this gap in quality. Sporting Lisbon is one of the leading teams in Europe as youth teams are concerned, but that should be a target for LFC. And I am afraid money cannot be the answer in the U19 level. The Academy has great coaches and scouting team, so they need to analyze and improve. I for one trust Segura, Borrell, and the rest of them. Surely they all have "A wish for something more" (yet again, Amy MacDonald).

This NextGen tournament can be extremely beneficial for the club and players in that they get confronted with the very best, they experience the level they are required to achieve, they see what they need to improve, and the coaches will figure out ways of how they can achieve that much needed improvement.

Youth football is not only about winning. But winning is part and parcel of the learning curve. As it is, more importantly, competing with the best, and testing yourself against them. In doing so, LFC can hopefully unearth in their ranks the "Next best thing", to finalise, as I started, with Amy MacDonald.

19.- Game-planning and team-comparing

Date: 24-November-2011
Previous results: Chelsea 1-2 LFC (Premier League); LFC Reserves 5-1 Sunderland Reserves

A lot of positives can be taken from the Chelsea game, no doubt. Some great individual performances and the result, to name just a few. But what stands out for me is having seen a team with a clear plan, knowing what to do, and when, and where, to do it. That is something that I for one have been missing for a while.

It is also worth noting that that was not the only good result this week, the 5-1 win against Sunderland reserves on Tuesday at the Academy adding to it. There is no comparing the importance of both results, obviously. But it has been a good chance to see how things are developing at reserve level.

And those matches in quick succession provide the fans with the opportunity to try an exercise of comparing and contrasting both teams. At least, I thought I wanted to try, first as a player by player basis; then, the teams as a whole.

To begin with, the goalkeepers; both had little to do in their games. Still, both solved well the problems, and both had at least one extremely good goalkeeping action. That is all, regarding the similarities. Reina saved a very difficult header in a defining moment in the match. Had it not been for that save, the game could have been very different. Hansen made a very good save with the game close to its end, and the result decided.

As for central defenders, both pairs did a fairly good account of themselves. Agger and Skrtel coped well with Chelsea forwards, and often helped to play the ball through the midfielders. Wilson and Coates had not much to do, and Coates even scored. As for left backs, Enrique had a more quiet game than usual, but he controlled well defensively; Wisdom made a handful of good runs in attack, although he showed some difficulties in defence.

As holding midfielders, Leiva and Coady had good games, but neither of them had their best games. They were solid, composed, they helped their defenders, but both have had better games on the ball. Different story for Adam and Spearing. Adam gave a man of the match performance, bossing the game for long spells, and displaying the player we all want him to be. Let's hope he can build on this performance and grow as a player. Spearing scored twice, and showed great resolution in running on the attack, and shooting at goal. This game would have done him no harm, in his confidence and ability to run a team and help in attack.

On the wings, Kuyt and Maxi were not brilliant, but they contributed a great deal to the game plan (and, obviously, Maxi scored again), preventing Chelsea defenders and midfielders from being comfortable on the ball, causing all sorts of troubles to them, and recovering the ball very often. Sterling had a very different task, and he was not very fortunate; he tried tirelessly, which is a good sign, but it was not his game. On the other side, and very often through the middle, Suso had another very good game, after the week before in the NextGen Series match. He was a nightmare for

Sunderland defenders, read well the match, and was very assured when in possession.

In the hole behind the strikers ("between the lines", as said Benitez), Bellamy had a very good game, pressing, running, opening spaces, combining,...He is increasingly making his case for more minutes in the first team, and he could be an extremely valuable asset for the season. Adorjan did not play well. He could hardly find his place during the game, and did not perform at his level. Suarez and Morgan had similar games. Both tried, but were not fortunate. Nothing to reproach them for in terms of effort, but they were not lucky. Suarez seemed a bit tired after what has been a very busy start to the season.

I have left the right backs until the end. Johnson, of course, decided the game with his goal, a great action, choosing the right moment for running into the space, and managing brilliantly the situation. Not to forget the contribution of Adam with his inch-perfect pass. Beyond the goal, Johnson showed increasing signs of getting back to his best; he had some problems defending, but he looked comfortable on the ball, and involved in the game. With the reserves, Flanagan was simply outstanding. He run, dribbled, shoot, passed,...he did everything, and was head and shoulders over the rest of the players. Very pleasant headache for Dalglish, having Johnson, Kelly and Flanagan at his disposal.

Finally, the substitutes, amongst whom Eccleston shone. He was different class, scoring twice in few minutes and conveying a feeling of absolute superiority. Hopefully he can play some minutes in Stamford Bridge next week.

The collective performance of both teams was good. But, as said before, not every player was at their best. There is clear room for improvement in both cases, which bodes well for the future. The reserves were somewhat inconsistent, with brilliant spells and moments with lower rhythm.

The first team had a great game-plan during the first half, in which Chelsea were almost completely nullified. Closing spaces in the central areas, pressing up in the pitch, looking for recovering the ball the moment the opposition defenders were experiencing difficulties (as epitomised in the first goal), and very importantly, outnumbering and outplaying Chelsea in midfield,...LFC run the game in every aspect, and only the lack of some edge in the attacking box prevented them from scoring more goals.

However, the first 20/25 minutes of the second half were a completely different story. Whatever the reason, LFC opted for (or were obliged to) defend much closer to Reina's goal, and with way less pressure on Chelsea players; and two things you should never give to Chelsea players are space and time. It was in this moments were it came the "saving save" by Reina, but the defeat loomed over LFC for certain time.

Credit to the players, though, they were able to come back, regroup and turn again the game to their benefit, which is a very difficult thing to do during a game, capping the performance with that great goal and victory.

It is important to have a game-plan, and LFC controlled the game when their players were able to impose their plan, whereas Chelsea were in command when they were able to impose theirs. The fact that LFC had around 65/70 minutes of control, and Chelsea only 20/25, proved ultimately key to the final score.

During this season I have been able to identify a clear game-plan in the matches against Arsenal, ManU and Chelsea, but I could not see it against Norwich, Swansea,…, maybe except some short spells, mostly at the beginning of the matches. I want to stress that, obviously, my not seeing of the plan does not imply that the plan does not exist. Anyway, I like to decipher the plans, and I hope next match against Man City will be one in which I can see the game-plan.

20.- First and second units tested

Date: 2-December-2011
Previous results: LFC 1-1 ManCity (Premier League);
Chelsea 0-2 LFC (Carling Cup)

In the last few days we have had the opportunity to see in action most of the LFC 2011/2012 squad. While what we could consider the "first unit" confronted Man City on Sunday, the "second unit" was called into action in Stamford Bridge on Tuesday. Overall, a fairly satisfactory balance, more in terms of the quality of play than in terms of the scores, given the undeserved draw against City.

There was no second unit in goal, with Reina playing both games. He had hardly anything to do in Stamford Bridge, but was busier against City, though often through his own defenders and their passes, more dangerous than City forwards. Good games for Reina. As right backs, Johnson and Kelly performed well. Maybe one could have expected a little bit more from Johnson, who had Nasri and Clichy, not the best defenders in the world, in front of him. Kelly wanted to prove that if Johnson could score in Stamford Bridge, so could he. Very good sign, the defenders starting to add goals.

Central defenders were excellent. I have been very critical to them, and still think it is an area in which additions are needed. But in those games all four did phenomenally well. Maybe it was Coates who excelled, looking unsurpassable and composed. No changes in left back, either, with Jose Enrique at his usual solid displays. He seems to have lost a little bit of spark going forward, but continues to be a very reliable defender and player.

In midfield Leiva kept his trend of improving, only to end up being badly injured. A real shame, and hopefully he will come to his best after the long recovery. Best wishes to him. By his side, Adam and Spearing. Adam is getting better over the last few games. Even so, he needs to step up his ruling of the games; he needs to be at the centre of everything during the matches. As of now, he has brilliant spells along with phases in which he is missed. But he is on a high now, getting to know his team-mates, coaches, club,...and becoming a better player. Spearing had a good game. Probably one problem of him is the lack of competitive games that have made him unconfident and lacking rhythm and knowledge of the other players. He may get more games from now on, which would help improve his game.

On the wings we have seen many players, with many changes of positions during games. More remarkable issues in my view: Downing is still struggling to adjust, he cannot find his form, and is losing confidence: his shoots at goal are worsening; he probably needs a goal more than anyone in the team. On the contrary, Maxi cannot stop scoring; I have to admit I don't see him as a particularly great player: he is not quick, not very skilful, not a good dribbler,...but he certainly knows how to score, and the team needs that. Kuyt works endlessly, as always, but this season has yet to find his game. Henderson looks far more comfortable on the middle than on the wing. There is a problem in the right wing; apparently the aim is to get several players interchanging positions during games, but it is confusing much more LFC players than the opposition. Either the players and staff need to work on this in training, or they need to find another solution.

Tellingly, the best player at right wing was Bellamy, who played there for only a few minutes and made Maxi's goal. Bellamy is proving to be a more than able player, a great asset to the team, whether as a winger in either side or as a second striker. I find it difficult to understand why he tends to be the first substituted, though there must be a reason for that.

As strikers, Suarez and Carroll are kind of opposite cases. Suarez is a headache for the defenders no matter what he does. In the last few games he looks somewhat tired, which is understandable. Even so, he keeps trying, running, pressing,…and manages to be dangerous even when playing badly (or not particularly well). Carroll, on the other hand, seems to have a dark cloud over him, and plays badly even when he plays well. No matter how hard he tries, and he tries very hard, everything seems to end up the wrong way. The penalty against Chelsea could have helped turn it around, but it didn't. However, the lad has quality, and hopefully it will come good sooner rather than later.

All in all, two good team performances. The match against City started poorly, and changed after those two goals. It was odd, to certain extent; theoretically, the score were very much the same in minutes 30 (0-0) and 35 (1-1); however, the match changed dramatically, for the benefit of LFC. Since then, the LFC ruling of the game was growing, and the victory was largely deserved. Significant was that moment, in 89th minute, when Silva found himself in front of Reina and waited, and waited, and finally had to shoot with not least than three LFC players on the line to collect the ball, while not even one City player was anywhere near. Clearly, one team was looking for the victory and the other was only waiting for the match to end.

The Carling Cup game confronted two second units, as it were. And LFC's second unit proved to be widely superior to Chelsea's. LFC dominated the game from the go, with only short spells of allowing Chelsea in the game. By far, the worst news for LFC was Leiva's injury; other than that, the team was always in command and the victory was almost a foregone conclusion, given the run of play. Even so, I didn't quite like the last minutes, in which LFC simply waited in his own half. But a more than satisfactory performance, overall. The team showed certain difficulties related to the lack of experience in playing together. That should be taken into account when judging the display; it is one thing to include a couple of players into a well functioning team, and it is a completely different thing to change almost the whole team. In this case a lot of mechanisms of playing are missing, and the players need to adjust during the game. But they did it well.

LFC have more than proved than they are able to compete against the best teams around. Let's hope they find a way to confront the Norwiches, the Swanseas, the Blackburns, and, beginning this coming Monday, the Fulhams, and not only the ManUs, the Chelseas, and the Arsenals.

I want to end sending my best wishes to Leiva in his recovering process; and, of course, my deepest condolences to all the many relatives and friends of Gary Speed, a true football legend.

21.- Einstein and balanced assessment

Date: 8-December-2011
Previous results: Fulham 1-0 LFC (Premier League)

After the disappointment of the Fulham result, at least two main trends can be seen between LFC fans: on the one hand, the total despair of "here we go again, losing against minor teams, we will never get to where we belong..."; on the other hand, the delusional "never mind, nothing to worry about, only bad luck in scoring chances, things will come our way...".

Obviously, the vast majority of fans belong somewhere between those extreme positions. As do I. So I wanted to offer my views on the meaning of that game. Being my views, I think of them as "balanced", though I am well aware that any of you see your own opinions likewise. But, for what it is worth, here is my take.

To begin with the undisputable, LFC lost the game, which is hardly good news; nearly (not totally) as undisputable, LFC did more than enough to win (at the very least, not to lose) the game. The sheer truth is that this is not the first time it happens to LFC in recent times. So there must be something that could, and needs to, be done to fix it. Otherwise, we are condemned to find ourselves in this position time and time again.

LFC players need to be more clinical in front of the opposite goal, no doubt about that. To that end, do LFC need to sign one or two more strikers? To devote specific training sessions to developing those skills? To bring in a new goal scoring coach? Or simply do nothing but wait until everything clicks in and the issue is solved? I don't have the answers. Having been Dalglish himself one of the better finishers you can find, he is surely thinking of it, and I hope he can find a way out.

As for the building of the attacking game, I think there is still a problem in the right wing. For any reason, Kuyt does not quite click in this season the way he did in the former seasons; Henderson looks lost there; and when in the last games it has been tried to rotate players during the game, they seem confused. I can think of two possible answers for this: playing there Glen Johnson to take advantage of his attacking skills, or Bellamy, who looked great there against Chelsea and could perform in the long term. Or maybe putting more work in training ground might result in that rotation of different players interchanging their positions during games working out.

The defensive side of the game seems to be solid as of now. It took a while, but it is working now, not only in terms of not receiving many goals, but also in terms of not allowing many scoring chances to the opposition. I for one would prefer to see a partnership of Carragher and Agger, but I have to admit that Skrtel is playing fine at the moment, despite his remaining irritating costume of trying to clear aerial balls with his feet on the ground.

What should really be assessed is the goalkeeping. There is not arguing Reina is a great goalkeeper, and has been an outstanding servant to the club. But his mistakes are costing points. Against Fulham it was not a case of "bad luck mistake", a rebound that could have gone either way. It was poor goalkeeping. The way he went for the ball had no other possible end that the way it ended. Again, he has won many points for the team, so it is not a case of going after him. But it would be great to find the reasons of these last episodes of lacking of focus. Maybe the captaincy has something to do with it? I don't know, but the team needs the better Reina back.

On the plus side, there is undoubtedly the defensive side of the team. The back four seems to have clicked and look pretty solid. It has come at the cost of less attacking involvement by the full backs, which seem to be more selective in their running up the pitch. Of course, the defending is a task for every player, and not only the back four. In that sense, there is a challenge pending in the form of the injury to Leiva.

While he was on the pitch against Fulham, Spearing played well, and Leiva was not particularly missed. Then the sending off came (harsh red card, in my view), and the team was not able to fully react. I saw encouraging signs of Spearing, and this red card and the suspension could be really damaging to him and the team. Given a decent run of games, Spearing would probably settle in and do his work for the team. As the things are now, something has to be figured out for the coming games: playing Agger in midfield, giving a chance to Shelvey or Coady, pairing Adam with Henderson,...It will be interesting to see the choice made.

Saving that problem with the injury of Leiva, the midfield is doing a very good work in the last games defensively. Not so good, but good enough, in supporting the attack. Still, goals are missing. But the pressure on the opposition defence is getting better and better, and that is one of the keys to a top team, stopping the rival game from the very beginning. The work on this pressure up the pitch, on the defenders of the opposition, is paying off, and should the team stay that course we will probably see more rewards of that approach. The pressure is much helped by the strikers, which are working their socks off in helping the team. They need more luck and more accuracy in scoring, but are contributing to the team and playing their part.

To sum up, the structure of the team looks solid, the lines and players are closer than weeks ago, they all work on the field as a unit, and the opposite teams find it very difficult to play against LFC. Not that the team is playing defensively; this structure works on the attack, too, and the midfield try to dictate the game and dominate the run of play, which they have accomplished on almost every of last 4/5 games. Plus, a serious improvement can be seen, and the team is growing and getting better.

The immediate challenge is to keep that progression without Leiva for the season, and his natural replacement for next few games. And, more generally, to make that structure count on the opposition box; more specifically, on the opposition goal. Create more goal chances and elevate the conversion rate.

It is good to acknowledge the good things the team is doing, and keep them going. But, as Einstein allegedly once said, it is "insanity doing the same thing over and over again and expecting different results". So let's hope the team keeps up the good work they are doing, and figure out how to improve in the areas needed. Coming matches are of the "easy" type, and that type has proved to be very difficult for the team, so the opportunity for showing improvement is there.

22.- *Looking for theories*

Date: 14-December-2011
Previous results: LFC 1-0 QPR (Premier League)

Like many football fans, I enjoy having clear theories about what is going on, what are the main traits of the players, what are the explanations for what is going right or wrong,…I must admit that one of the unanswered questions for me used to be the goalscoring profligacy of Maxi Rodriguez.

Don't get me wrong. He was (and is) a good, competent, player, no doubt about that. But no matter how hard I looked into him, I couldn't quite understand that level of goals; he is not the quickest player, he is not the toughest shooter of the ball, he is not particularly skilful,…So, why was it that he couldn't stop scoring?

Obviously, nothing I was willing to complain about. As an LFC fan, I am more than happy to welcome as many a goals as Maxi wants to score. But, as said above, I tend to look for some kind of explanations of footballing facts. He is experienced, knows about football, knows how, when, and where to move,…but I couldn't help thinking that all those traits didn't account for that amount of goals.

Well, at least I have now an additional theory. It was Menotti, the 1978 World Cup winner as manager of the Argentina national team, who coined the Spanish term "pequeña sociedad", which can be translated into English as something like "small partnership".

Those small partnerships are the playing relationships developed on the pitch between two players that, somehow, seem to have an understanding far superior to the usual one. A well known example is that of Maradona/Burruchaga in Mexico '86, where they didn't need to look at each other to know what to do in order to do damage to the opposition.

Of course, that kind of almost telepathy is not by any means unknown to LFC fans. Some examples come to mind immediately: Keegan/Toshack, Dalglish/Rush, Barnes/Beardsley,...Over the last years, that Gerrard/Torres of the 2008/2009 season falls in that category.

And many others, especially in terms of attacking pairs. The normal examples are between two strikers, a striker and the man on the hole, or a striker and a wing. However, I like also those pairs more defensive, or less attacking, like Alonso/Mascherano, who seemed to complement each other almost perfectly. And one of my favourites, which I know is not particularly popular, Hansen/Hysen.

So, what has all of the "small partnership" to do with Maxi? Well, many of you have probably guessed that I am starting to thing that Suarez/Maxi are forging one of those partnerships. During the QPR game, Suarez and Maxi, not for the first time, found themselves time and again in menacing positions, and were at times almost unreadable for the defenders. Meanwhile, Kuyt was like the unexpected guest, failing to really make a meaningful connection with Suarez or Maxi.

That is not to say that Kuyt did anything wrong. He worked, as usual, tirelessly, and helped the team to the best of his ability. But, as a striker in a team that ruled the game for the 90 minutes, he had little chances and influence, at least compared with Maxi. One such partnership can be developed, or at least enhanced, on the training pitch, but generally there is something elusive, almost mysterious, in it. Managers, and other players, have to detect, encourage, and put to the benefit of the team those partnerships.

Having said that about Maxi and his involvement in the game, what stood out was undoubtedly the performance by Suarez. It was almost out of this world, head and shoulders above the rest of players. I couldn't agree more with QPR player (and LFC fan) Bradley Orr, who said that Suarez was "unplayable". That was the kind of display that raises (yet again) those opinions of one-man team. But, for now, I am sick and tired of that issue (to which I might come back at any point, who knows), so I will simply acknowledge the great game Suarez had.

As for the rest of the team, the defenders were at their usual good of last games. As far as I know, no well known manager has said anything about a name for a small (or big) partnership of four, but certainly these string of games in which Johnson, Skrtel, Agger, and Enrique have been able to play together in succession have done the world of good to them and the team.

Adam kept up his good work, dictating the play from the midfield, with a good range of passes; not really brilliant, I think, but good game, though I still think that there should be more to come from him. Henderson did his job, in difficult circumstances, given that he had to play much more as a "holding" that as a "midfielder". He may get accustomed to that position but, for now, he is simply a last resource. Downing has yet to find his best form; meanwhile, he is doing his part, but a much better Downing is needed.

All in all, the team played well, but the path to converting the superiority in goals is still missing, and need to be found sooner rather than later for the team to have a successful season. As of now, the defenders, Adam and Suarez are sustaining the team; they all need help from their teammates. But, while building a team, a win is a huge help. A convincing win against Villa next Sunday will help the improvement process that is in progress.

And many fans will accompany that process with sometimes well founded, and other times blatantly unfounded, theories, like that one of the "small partnerships".

23.- Learning curve

Date: 19-December-2011
Previous results: Aston Villa 0-2 LFC (Premier League)

Just before the kick-off yesterday I had a certain feeling that it could be a good match for LFC; the team had been growing during the previous weeks, the players looked focused, Bellamy was in the starting eleven, and it seemed as the perfect occasion for Downing to finally rise up his level against his former team-mates.

However, not in my wildest dreams could I have hoped for such a starting to the game. At 15th minute, that was an absolute demolition of the opposition. That 2-0 looked just the beginning, with LFC players unstoppable for Villa defenders and midfielders, and Villa forwards...well, there seemed to be no one at all. At least in my telly. Those 15 minutes may stand as one of the models for this team, at least when playing these types of games, away games against theoretically inferior opponents. Playing like that, there will be no Bolton, no Blackburn, no Fulham, no Sunderland,...able to take away points from LFC.

The defenders were not only solid, but dominant, not allowing the opposition even the thought of a chance of getting near the goal. Moreover, they assured the possession, either moving themselves to the midfield, if necessary, either passing the ball to the best placed team-mate. The midfielders kept the ball moving to the zones of the pitch where it would be more damaging to the rivals. And the forwards were constantly moving around, interchanging positions, to the point Villa defenders were left with no option but to raise their hands and surrender.

Capped with a couple of goals, the performance was nearly perfect. It was perhaps not spectacular, not exactly brilliant, but clinically precise and accurate. All that remained for the fans in our homes was to keep seated and wait for the goals to follow up.

But…No goals followed up. After 20 minutes, give or take, the team decided to bank on the two goals cushion and simply wait for the minutes to pass. From then to halftime, they stopped pressing the Villa defenders, allowed the Villa midfielders time and space, and focused on keeping the clean sheet. And so they did. Reina had no part in the game whatsoever, so the win was never in danger. The three points were all but secured. It was what at time it is called a "professional performance".

And then it came the halftime. And, as it is always the case, the second half. And there was again. The same LFC of the beginning of the match, maybe even better. For around another 20 minutes or so, one of the best displays we have seen from a Liverpool team in several months, if not years. That was a title winning team.

How the score was still 2-0 at 65th minute was beyond understanding of everyone involved, particularly certain unstoppable player by the name of Luis Suarez. Not that is was a perfect performance; some of the players were to some extent below their best. But that is only normal. The team as a whole was great over those minutes. Surely now the goals would follow?

No, they wouldn't. Pretty much like what happened in the first half, the team opted to sit back and simply wait, with the odd exception in the form of isolated contra-attacks, but with no pressing defence, with the line just on the edge of Reina's box. Nothing really damaging happened. The match was under control all the time, and Reina have not had a more quiet game for quite a time.

What I wonder is to what extent these ups and downs were planned, maybe saving for the hectic schedule ahead, and to what extent the case is that the team is not yet ready to keep the pace for longer periods of time. Difficult to know, I suppose, but the stark contrast between the first and second part of each half was as remarkable as it gets.

Also remarkable was getting no less that two goals from set pieces. And neither of those was kicked by Adam, who had been the main taker of them before. This time, Downing and especially Bellamy caused danger with their crosses. Good to know that the resources are there for the team to take advantage.

However, after those two quick goals the team found yet again its usual difficulties to transform the chances in goals. Not serious this time, but it has cost in previous matches, and surely everyone at Anfield is doing their best to improve the conversion rate. Something that needs to be done.

Regarding individual performances, I have already highlighted Luis Suarez. In what was a very good performance, some players underperformed a bit, though; Adam was slightly below their last games, which is only worrying if, and only if, it was to certain extent due to the amount of matches he has played; does he need a rest? Enrique was also a bit shy in his going forward.

Henderson needs to learn about this new position in which he is playing now. Sometimes he gives away the ball by taking excessive risks, playing as a holding midfielder. And Downing, after a brilliant start to the game, looked unconfident and lost at times. The lad works hard, no doubt, but has yet to find his best form.

On the bright side, besides Suarez, I would like to mention Bellamy, causing all sorts of problems to the defenders; Shelvey, who starred in a difficult role in his first game of the season for LFC, leaving very promising signs. And a very especial mention to Glen Johnson, who was great, both defending and attacking; dribbling and passing; playing short and long balls. He keeps growing and could be key to the season if he can keep his improving course.

All in all, a very encouraging performance. The team needs to work on that beginning of both halves, and keep the level for longer spells. In doing so, they will have found a way to face the low tier teams, which have been the difficult ones during last seasons, in which more than a once promising path have come to an abrupt end in one of those so called "easy" games. In the near future, I will keep a close eye on the Wigan match, to check if the improving process continues, if the learning curve goes on.

24.- The same old story, same old act

Date: 23-December-2011
Previous results: Wigan 0-0 LFC (Premier League)

Something occurs time and again in last seasons, to the point the fans are not even taken by surprise: the team plays three or four good games, gets a handful of good results, shows some progress, some signals of being growing, getting back to the good old times,...and then slips down in some "easy" game.

It may be a bad refereeing decision; an injury to a key player; a last minute goal against; a harsh sending off; or a failed penalty shoot. Some times the bad result is widely deserved, some times is a blatant injustice. But there is no hiding the constant feeling that every good run of matches and results looks bond to end every 3, 4, 5 matches.

There is no hiding the constant hope that at some moment that has to end, either. The game against Wigan was one of those games, at least for me, but I tend to think that for a number of other LFC fans, too.

The game against Aston Villa left the LFC staff and fans in a fairly optimistic mood; though far from a perfect display, it was a solid performance, with some great minutes of play. So we all faced the Wigan game in expectation, and hoping for a confirmation that the growing process of the team stayed its course.

Alas, it was not to be. Admittedly, the game started very well for LFC. The players looked sharp, pressing the opposition defenders to the extent Wigan could hardly get into the LFC half. For nearly 20 minutes, or so, the team seemed to have drawn the correct lessons from the game at Villa Park.

At that point, a goal could come every moment. For those 20 minutes, the defence was seldom called into action, the midfield circulated the ball well towards the wings and forwards, and the constant movement of Suarez, Maxi, Downing and Kuyt was too much for the Wigan defenders.

However, it is true that no really clear-cut chances appeared. LFC were not getting even in the state of squandering goal chances. But the feeling was that, should they keep playing like that, that would surely be corrected in almost no time.

Or maybe not that surely. Having followed the good path set by the Villa match, the players also followed the bad one. At around 20 minutes, the play started to vanish. Suddenly, the Wigan defenders were able to take the ball to the midfielders, the midfielders found time and space to play, and the game began to be played more on the LFC half.

Not that Wigan were by any means superior to LFC, but certainly they were not inferior, either. The match was flat, the minutes passing without real highlights to show. The ball was going up and down the pitch with little purpose, and no real authority was stamped on the match.

When the half-time came, LFC could only hope for the players to keep following what happened at Birmingham, where the start to the second half was again brilliant, and the goal chances flooded. Regrettably, that was not the case against Wigan.

The team showed some more ambition in the first stages of the second half, trying to grab that most needed victory. But the inspiration, the quality of play, the accuracy of the ball handling, were simply not there. Even so, a penalty came LFC way after a good overhead kick by Suarez. On the telly, it seemed as if Suarez asked to take it himself, but it was Adam who did. After Al-Habsi stopped the penalty, there were still more than 30 minutes remaining, but just like in the first half, the game turned flat, dull, and sparkless.

It was only in the dying moments of the match that LFC suddenly came into life and increased the search for the winning goal, but it was too little (or too much) too late. In the end, a disappointing draw, that does not help the team to climb the table to where they should be.

Not that everything was down-heartening. The team kept its consistency at the defence. The back four seem to be more and more solid as the games passes. I am starting to be afraid that Reina will begin to get even bored during matches. And that is a pretty good thing for a team. As long as the defence is solid, there is a basis for the building of the team.

In the midfield there are more problems. Henderson, as hard as he tries, is not a natural holding midfielder, and has problems in his decisions, resulting in the team losing rhythm, and failing to dictate the game for long spells. He may improve with more matches and time in training ground, spent in that position, though I am not sure the team can afford that time; or maybe the return of Spearing can help with that.

Adam looks a little bit worn out. He has probably played too much without a rest, and is suffering. Whether it is more a mental or a physic problem, I couldn't say. But he may need one or two matches out in order to come back to his best. Again, the problem is whether the team can afford it.

Downing keeps struggling to find his form. He tries, no doubt about that. But, as of now, he is not helping the team as much as he should, as much as his known quality makes us expect. Kuyt has not really kick-started his season. He looks as if running and playing in a different team, as if he is not fully adapted to the current team.

Bellamy, Maxi and Suarez are playing well, with their logic ups and downs, but they are having a good season. However, if LFC is going to have a really good season, Carroll is needed, and a way has to be found to bring him into the team.

Meanwhile, next Monday there is another chance to start a good run of games, that hopefully will this time last more than the usual 3,4 matches. The potential is there, the quality is there. Probably it is only a little bit of luck what is being missed. But, after the last disappointment, I can't help thinking that it was the LFC team of last seasons in which Bruce Springsteen was thinking when he wrote, in his song "One step up", about him being "the same old story, same old act, one step up and two steps back".

25.- Back to basics

Date: 28-December-2011
Previous results: LFC 1-1 Blackburn (Premier League)

It was none other than the great Bill Shankly himself who once stated: "Above all, the main aim is that everyone can control a ball and do the basic things in football". This piece of wisdom, much related in my view to past Blackburn game, also applies to other sports.

Those of you who are (or were) basketball fans, are likely to remember the time (end of 80's, beginning of 90's) in which basketball players from what then was Yugoslavia were the dominant force in Europe (if not further).

It was often said that the key to that dominance was the training methods for kids and youngsters. In Yugoslavia, we were told time and again, the emphasis was put in the players being comfortable with the ball, and with all the basic operations with it.

Thus, a Yugoslavian basket player was likely to know how to keep the ball, how to pass it, and how to throw at basket. Those were the basics of basketball. From there, a player would grow up to step up his game, and eventually become a really great player, by having real talent for the game, learning to do more complex movements, to play in a team, being a strong character,...

But every player, being a star or being what in English football we would call a "Sunday league" player, would know the basics of the game. I cannot know the extent of the accuracy of this theory, but at least it is well founded, it makes sense. And the now Serbian, Croatian, Bosnian,...basket players are still amongst the best in the world.

I for one was reminded of these ideas during the Blackburn game. The quality of passes, and especially crosses and shots, from LFC players was really appalling. Lots of somewhat well constructed actions were squandered by a terrible, terrible, pass, cross, or shot. And those are part of what one may consider "basics" of football.

Every football player should know how to deliver a short-range pass to a team-mate. After all, that was the very basic of Shankly game: give the ball to the nearest red shirt, and run to where you can get the ball again. But in the game against Blackburn there were some passes really difficult to understand. Easy, routine passes that went out of the pitch with little, or none, justification.

Even more frustrating, for me, were the crosses. The contribution of good crosses to good football is beautifully expressed by LFC fan QuinnsRed in his profile in The Kop social network, where he writes: "Steve Heighway running down the wing dodging tackles, crossing with pin point accuracy to Toshack and Keegan ..The rest is history...".

During the Blackburn game, the team managed to get a decent amount of good crossing positions, in which Johnson, Enrique, Downing, Suarez,...got some space and time to deliver the ball to the box. And time and again the crosses either felt extremely short at the feet of defenders or went far beyond the box. There were, of course, some exceptions, but the cross accuracy was way below what it should be.

This inability to turn good movements and passing-game into good crosses was particularly pitiful in the case of Downing. He may have had one of his best LFC games, and looked unstoppable for the Blackburn defenders, but to little real effect on the game. He ran, dribbled, got pass players, as often as one may wish. But then he either was fouled or his cross was poor. Many chances-to-be got frustrated this way. Similarly with the rest of players that got into crossing positions. Not that any single cross was poor, but the rate of good crosses was extremely low. Which is particularly costing for a team that is prepared to carry out its attack through the wings.

And also disappointing were the shots at goal. According to eplindex.com, 22 shots, only 7 on target (and one goal). That is even poorer than the season average to date. And let's not forget that the statistics were improved by those two late efforts by Carroll and Agger. Sometimes, whatever the reason, the players seem to lack the ability to properly shot the ball. Now, I (and every fan) know that this cannot be the case, given they are proven first level players.

But, really, the amount of times the ball goes directly to the stands is remarkable. Particularly, over the cross bar, which indicates, generally speaking, a poorly executed shot. Difficult as I find to blame it on the quality of the players, I also find it difficult to blame it solely on bad luck. There must be something else, be it the tension, the pressure, the lack of confidence, lack of practice,...I don't know, I don't watch the trainings, I don't know the players.

So it is maybe time for a back-to-basics approach. I am sure the players know how to pass, how to cross, how to shot. But they might need to refocus on these basics. A slight improvement on those basic abilities would have been more than enough to comfortably beat Blackburn.

Having said that, the team played sufficiently well to have won the game; created enough chances to have won the game; would have won the game 9 out of 10 times; deserved to win the game; was much better than the opposition. This much is true, and I agree. But it should also not be forgotten what was that opposition, maybe the worst team seen at Anfield for a long time, injury-plagued, with young debutants, extremely tired for the last part of the game,...Even if any of those last chances had gone in, and the match had been won, a deep reflection would have been needed.

If the club and the fans keep speaking only about the bad luck, and the great opposition goal-keepers (which, by the way, was not the case in the last game except for that late save to Carroll), we are unlikely to see improvements. The players are not playing to their own standards, and a reason has to be found and solved. Maybe some of them need a rest; maybe they need specific training; maybe they need time to relax and free their minds; maybe they need confidence; maybe an adjustment in tactics is needed; maybe a reinforcement in the basics of football.

Even the great Yugoslavian basket players had the odd bad game, the odd defeat, the odd bad pass, the odd bad shot. But the basics were there, meaning they would come back in no time. These LFC players and staff have proven to be capable of much more than we have seen in last matches. Newcastle will provide them with a chance for raise up their game and, hopefully, their results.

26.- Year ending, year beginning

Date: 1-January-2012
Previous results: LFC 3-1 Newcastle (Premier League)

In one of the scenes of a great Argentinean movie, *Luna de Avellaneda*, we can see a meeting of the organizers of a neighbourhood social club, in which the chairman asks the rest of the attendants to welcome a new addition, a good-looking girl. One after another, the directors welcome her and wish her a good time in the club. When the turn comes to one of the organizers, he says the usual "Welcome", and the girl answers with the usual "Thank you". But this guy emphasizes, "No, no, I mean *a very, very, warm* welcome", meaning of course that his "welcome" was not a routine one. He really meant it, and he was more than happy to have her there, to the extent that a mere "Welcome" was not enough to express it.

Now, I was reminded of this scene when the results of this last Premier League gameweek were coming through. After the LFC win over Newcastle, those Man City loss, ManU loss, Chelsea loss, Tottenham draw,...made for an excellent way to end 2011 and begin 2012. And I mean, not just excellent, but *extremely, extremely*, excellent. All that was missing was the result at the Emirates, but I guess that it would have been too much to ask for.

A 2011 that has been very eventful for LFC, mainly with the return of Dalglish to the helm of the squad. But also with a great change in the squad, and the technical staff. When it comes to the objective facts, Dalglish took the reins with the club having totalled 25 points in the 20 first games of 2010/2011, whereas, as of now, the total tally is 34 points in 19 games. A clear improvement from that point of view. In that sense 2012 begins much better than 2011.

On the other hand, it is as true that under Dalglish the team got 34 points in the remaining 18 games of last season, and, as said above, as many points in one more game in 2011/2012. In that sense, thus, the improvement has remained, but not gone further. All in all, Dalglish has taken charge of the team in 37 league games (almost a whole season) amassing 68 points. Good enough to mount a serious challenge for 4th spot, but far from aiming at the title.

I am the first to say that the mere numbers don't tell everything. After all, if data were all that mattered, any analysis and post like this would be deemed redundant. Data need to be properly analysed, and the correct conclusions properly dragged. That said, in my view the points in the league, before and after the summer, explain the basic state of the squad fairly well: a clear improvement has taken place, but it is still a work in progress; more has to be done, in terms of players, of consistency, of level of play, of results.

The club can put its sights on a 4th spot as a realistic aim for this season, given where it is coming from; but in the long term, be it two, three, four seasons, the aim can be no other than a title challenging team. The task is undoubtedly a difficult one, competing against, amongst other obstacles, the endless money of Man City and Chelsea owners; but the greatness is the reward for difficult achievements, not easy ones.

The hard question to answer, the one the bare data do not respond, is whether the club is moving in the right track towards keeping the growing process or not. 34 points from 18 games were more than good enough for last season. 34 points from 19 games in current season are about enough, but indicate a certain lack of speed in the progress, after all the activity in the summer transfer window.

On the other hand, that same transfer activity accounts for a difficult period at the beginning of the season, so it is a fair expectation that the team could get better in the second half of 2011/2012. I have repeatedly expressed in these posts that I can see both good and bad signs, things I like very much in the team and things that I don't like at all.

All this hesitation and lack of clear ideas (from me, not the team) was well exemplified in the Newcastle game. At first sight, a 3-1 win against the 7th team of the table is a more than satisfying outcome. However, it was not a great game by LFC. There were very few goal chances, and little clarity in the game. On the other hand, the team begins to seem almost unbeatable. Reina had nothing to do, other than pick the ball from the net after a very unlucky own goal, and try to stop Ba from scoring in what ended in an almost superhuman goal-line clearance by Skrtel.

Skrtel and Agger were rock-solid. And Agger is getting more and more involved in ball-playing, which is an excellent sign I would very much like to see developed. Johnson and Enrique, as full backs, were good in defence, although they did not get forward as often as I would have liked. When they run forward they caused all sorts of problems to opposition defenders, but they both were quiet for long spells of the match.

In midfield, Adam seems more and more in need of rest. He had a great run of games around November, but now he is struggling to stamp his authority on the matches. Henderson looked far better when getting in attacking positions, not only but also in the 3rd goal. He is not comfortable as holding midfielder. On the contrary, Spearing played very well, and gave much needed balance to the team. He looked composed and solid, and might be very important in coming matches.

Downing and Carroll gave other more-of-the-same performances. They both run, tried, worked,...but had little luck. They both need a match-winning display to step up their games, feel important to the team. But they simply cannot find it, very often because of bad luck, as the new woodwork by Carroll showed.

Bellamy was lively, and dangerous, kept moving, offered passes and gave them, scored two goals,...good game by him, although not his best this season. His addition looks more and more a master stroke. Gerrard played for 30 minutes, and was great. He seems to give sense to the play of all the team. Always knows where to be, what to do, when to move,...a player of a different level. And his crosses can make Carroll happy, sooner than later.

To sum up, a great result in a not so great a match. Good performances by some of the players, improvement needed by others, and the team as a whole. A solid base to build on, but building needed.

As a football fan, I don't have as much as New Year resolutions as End of Season targets for the team. For 2011/2012 LFC premier league, my personal targets would be to get around 40 points in the second half of it, thus totalling in the region of 75 points, and achieving the top four. And hopefully at least one trip to Wembley.

Other than that, my best wishes for 2012 to all LFC fans, and for Liverpool Football Club.

27.- Charming players

Date: 7-January-2012
Previous results: ManCity 3-0 LFC (Premier League); LFC 5-1 Oldham Ath. (FA Cup); LFC U18 1-0 Crewe U18

Although it goes against all logic, I cannot help thinking that there are certain football players that have something special on them. Players that, since they are still up-and-coming, seem to be unable of make mistakes. More precisely, players that seemingly always make meaningless mistakes and meaningful right moves.

Some of them have played for Liverpool Football Club, conspicuously certain Kenny Dalglish, who followed in the footsteps of another number seven as Kevin Keegan, who in his days also fell into this category. From the moment they got to the pitch as LFC players they started to score goals, be influential during games, and catch the eye of the fans, who almost immediately developed a liking to them.

Examples of such players can be found all over world football. Of the former Real Madrid and Spain national team star Raul, his first manager said that "you just shake him, and goals start to fall around". Another such player was the former Athletic Bilbao and also Spain national team star Julen Guerrero. In his first season with the first team, just a few days after his 19th birthday, he scored two goals in a 3-2 win. The opposition player who had to mark him said after the match: "He plays the ball OK, takes advantage of free zones, and has some skill inside the box, but, other than that, he was absolutely out of the game".

That is to say that sometimes these charming players are very difficult to decipher, by both journalists and fellow players. In these cases, their qualities are not always evident, and the pundits struggle to explain their success, at least in their first matches. Some players just get the tag of "charm" just for lack of properly understanding their game.

But that is not always the case. Other times, they are obviously brilliant players, quick, skilful, talented, and able to add to their brilliance that "something more" that makes them seem unstoppable. They can be at the right moment in the right place.

In their getting to LFC first team, Robbie Fowler and Michael Owen were such players. Certainly talented, certainly skilful, certainly brilliant players. But also with that ability to stole the show time and again, scoring for fun from the very beginning of their careers, and scoring special goals, decisive ones.

That "charm" was widely perceived by LFC supporters. And resisted the test of the passing of time, which is not always the case. It is very usual that almost every local player coming through the ranks of youth system to the first team is welcomed as one of these charming players. But very often the charm disappears after only few weeks, with the toughness of first team football.

I have been left thinking about all this after the U18 game this morning, LFC against Crewe. After a mostly uneventful match, more prone to a victory for Crewe than for LFC, five minutes from time, Jordan Lussey took the ball in midfield in an apparently routine situation. He advanced, looked around, didn't find good alternatives, and decided to shot from way outside the box. His shot, deflected by a Crewe player, was to become the only goal of the match.

This is not the first time Lussey finds the net in a significant moment, like his debut with the U18 team. I have barely seen him play, so I have no real idea if he is going to make it even to reserves level, but what he has achieved in his first half season with the U18 makes me think in a charming player, at least at that level. Only time will tell, though.

Not really charming in their first matches with LFC? Carroll and Downing. Both have been really struggling to find the form that led Dalglish to sign them. And both will hopefully benefit from the goals scored against Oldham in FA Cup.

They are different cases. Carroll arrived injured, and after a great amount of money paid by the club. He has hardly had a real run of games to get to know his new team, team-mates, city, environment,...And he has yet to adjust his game and to produce the amount of goals expected from a striker. Even so, he has scored for LFC about the same number of goals than Torres for Chelsea; and Torres has had way more minutes on the pitch. Incidentally, Torres scored more league goals for LFC (in one month) than for Chelsea (in eleven months) in 2011. Sometimes a transfer is a blessing in disguise; sometimes it is a curse in disguise.

Downing has played more than enough, apparently. But he cannot find his form. As a non-charming player, he runs, defends, tries, beats players, crosses,...but he has been mostly irrelevant, regarding his individual statistics. And failed to score one single goal until FA Cup arrived.

Both of them scored in the dying minutes of the match, and both were largely irrelevant goals. But each one can find some comfort in having scored. Carroll stamped the ball on the net a few moments after he entered the game. Downing managed to find a rebound and turn it into a goal. Both of them had previously failed to do so in similar circumstances, so hopefully they can find confidence in those achievements.

If so, the FA Cup game would have rendered a great service to LFC. It was not by any means a brilliant game, but the team went through, and found some missing goals. All things going well, the team would have found a path to the opposite net that may be put to good use in future games.

At least in the very near future, that would almost certainly need the involvement of Bellamy, who looks sharp, quick, clever,...a decisive player. Almost as decisive might be a full match-fit Gerrard, who might end up being the great January signing. A really charming signing in his own right.

28.- The way forward

Date: 22-January-2012
Previous results: ManCity 0-1 LFC (Carling Cup); LFC 0-0 Stoke (Premier League); Bolton 3-1 LFC (Premier League)

As many LFC fans, I was left extremely disappointed (to say the less) by the match against Bolton. It was not mainly the result, but the display, the apparent attitude, the level of play, the performance of the players. I am more than willing to accept a bad result if the performance is good enough. But not so willing to accept a bad performance even if the result is good. And much less to accept a bad result after an awful performance.

And that was what happened against Bolton. However, angry as I was, when considering what to write here in The Kop, I read what Dalglish had to say, and…I couldn't agree more with him. I couldn't be harder, or more explicit. I think that in this occasion Dalglish spoke for me, and probably for most of LFC fans. With one significant difference: I am not the manager of the team.

Dalglish's words reflected what happened on the pitch regarding the players and their performances. But I would also have liked to hear some word regarding the performance of the staff. Not only, nor mainly, to punish or derogate them (surely they did what they thought was better in that particular moment), but to find any indication that they know what caused the problems and are ready to sort it out, and prevent it from happening again in the future.

Anyway, I am not sure that everything can be blamed on the attitude or focus of the players. The team seems to be falling apart since several weeks ago. When on the pitch, the players look to have lost their purpose, their ideas, their know-how. Lack of reaction after those two early goals (one in each half) scored by one of the worst team of the league was appalling.

Receiving an early goal can be demoralising, but should be an opportunity to react with plenty of time. Not against Bolton. LFC never looked like getting back in the match. Not even after scoring a goal. Bolton was always the likeliest team to win the match, without even the shadow of a doubt. They ran out comfortable winners.

And that should be considered a flaw of the whole team, of the whole squad, including both the players and the staff. Lack of spirit goes beyond lack of quality, lack of preparation, lack of luck. I really hope, with Dalglish, that this has been a one time failure. Clearly unacceptable by LFC standards. If anything, an LFC team should show fight spirit, stamina, strength, will.

But we ought not to lose sight on the footballing side of things. If only commitment, fight spirit, and stamina would be enough, football would be a very different show. Many other qualities are needed, and current LFC squad seems to fall short on some of them.

First and foremost, there was no apparent game plan to be seen. Bolton players knew what to do, and what to try, in every moment; they have a clear plan on how to try and win the game. On the contrary, LFC players seemed completely lost, with no clue about what type of game should be played. Long balls? Pass and move? Attack through the wings? Through the middle? Deffend from the Bolton defence? Sit back and wait? Press aggressively on the bands? Or on the centre? Or not at all? There was not a pattern of play. Obviously, no team should play exactly the same during all game. But every team should know how to enter the game, and what are the tactics, beyond do-what-you-can-when-you-have-the-ball.

Surely the fact that the players did not seem to know the tactics doesn't equal the staff not having a game plan. But it is the type of question that needs to be addressed, apart from the apparent lack of commitment showed. The players need to reflect on the pitch the game plan the staff has developed. And especially they need not to look lost, both when in possession and when defending.

The club as a whole needs a clear way forward. One year into Dalglish reign, the team still lacks the consistency and the strength to really challenge for a top four spot, not to mention the title. Of course, there is a short-term way forward, which is waiting until Suarez ends his suspension. The team will improve then, and the results are likely to improve, too.

But looking deeper into the future, squad weaknesses need to be addressed and dealt with. And Bolton game was revealing in some aspects. The defence is both solid, if all the players remain fully focused in every moment, and fragile, the moment the focus is lost, even for a moment, like in those laughable goals against Bolton. More consistency is needed, especially in the centre of defence, where at least one top player is needed. Besides, Johnson and Jose Enrique should not be required to play every minute of every match; they are understandably tired by now, and they go forward much less times than they used to. As for Johnson, Kelly could provide some cover; it is much more difficult with Enrique.

In midfield, things are clearly not working by now. The team finds it almost impossible to take the ball from the back to the front by passing it between LFC players, and the midfielders are unable to really dictate and dominate the play during games. Henderson cannot play as right midfielder, where he is lost; Adam needs to dramatically improve his game if he is to be a proper LFC midfielder. Let's face it, Xabi Alonso is no longer an LFC player; but almost every team of the world play without Xabi Alonso in their ranks, so someone has to be found who can play his part. As of now, Spearing is by far the best option in the squad, so hopefully he will be available sooner that later. Probably Agger needs to get into midfield more often during games to help the midfielders. His getting in such positions was one of the very little good news against Bolton.

On the wings, Downing cannot find his form. He is potentially a good player, both on the right and on the left, but, whatever the reason, he cannot get to his best. And that is it, winger wise. Maxi is not really a winger, Kuyt, much as he works, has already given his best. So the only other option are Bellamy, who is excelling all expectations in every position, in every game, and Suarez, who can be deployed in either wing as a starting position. Not to forget, though, the option of playing Johnson as right wing.

As for strikers, there is Carroll, who seems to work hard, but to no avail. He simply cannot get himself into the team, so much work is needed for him to be really the striker of LFC. Even so, I still have some hopes with him. Only I don't know if the squad can allow the luxury of waiting for him.

I have not mentioned above the captain. Gerrard could of course fill many voids in the team. But, genius and outstanding player as he is, he cannot be the central midfielder, the holding midfielder, the right midfielder, the man in the hole, and the striker, all at the same time. He tried against Bolton, and the result was that he played one of his worst games in an LFC shirt.

So we all, including Dalglish, agree that the performance against Bolton was unacceptable. What is needed now is to take advantage of that performance in realistically assessing the situation and finding a path forward. For now, the immediate goal is to get to the Carling Cup final, which will be difficult but very rewarding. A trip to Wembley and a title would be a very good starting point for that way forward.

29.- Eight games later

Date: 1-February-2012
Previous results: LFC 2-2 ManCity (Carling Cup); LFC 2-1 ManUnited (FA Cup); Wolves 0-3 LFC (Premier League)

Finally, Luis Suarez has ended to serve his eight match ban, and he could come back to the pitch. So, what is the balance of those eight games for the team? Where were we before, and where are we after? What have we learnt about the team and squad?

Questions worth asking, I think. And worth trying to answer. Although almost any fan will have their own answer, I will try and find mine in next lines. Those eight games are exactly the games the team has played during January 2012. So, now in February it is a good moment to assess the team situation before the defining points of the season.

To begin with, the results. The eight matches have been divided between Premier League (4 games), Carling Cup (2 games) and FA Cup (2 games), a fairly interesting and assorted string of matches. As far as the Cups are concerned, nothing to complaint about. LFC qualified for the Carling Cup final, and for the 5th FA Cup round. So hundred per cent success on those fronts.

As for the League, the balance is not so good: one convincing win (3-0 away against Wolves), one disappointing draw (0-0 at Anfield against Stoke), one "normal" defeat (0-3 away against Man City) and one extremely embarrassing defeat (1-3 away against Bolton).

In terms of the results, then, LFC have had mixed fortunes. Very promising in the Cups, with one trip to Wembley already booked. The final with Cardiff is one every LFC fan will look to with hope in their hearts. It may be the first piece of silverware in almost six years, it will the first Wembley final in almost 16 years. It also might secure that European football returns to Anfield next year.

Another trip to Wembley is also possible in FA Cup, with both Manchester teams already off the competition and the team looking comfortable. Last round draw was hard, pairing LFC with ManU, but a match at Anfield against Brighton, who LFC already overcame this season in Carling Cup away, is hardly one to complaint about. However, the hardest stages of the competition are still ahead, so the Dalglish approach of one-game-at-a-time is surely the best way to handle it.

Hence, so far so good in Cups. The league is another story, though. Four points out of four games is hardly a satisfying outcome. LFC are still well in 4th spot race, but the team is still lacking consistency, and that aim looks now more difficult than a month ago, I reckon. Other teams in the race are also showing weaknesses, but sooner rather than later at least one of Chelsea, Arsenal, and LFC will find its form and start winning on a regular basis.

Next games are very difficult, on paper. Tottenham, ManU, Arsenal, and at some point Everton will pose a remarkable challenge. However, during past seasons the team has proven time and again to be more than able to confront the best teams. In that sense, the following string of nine games against so-called minor teams will probably be more decisive. Yet again, it is advisable to stick to that one-game-at-a-time philosophy.

So, results wise, January, with Suarez absence, has been as good as it gets in Cups, and LFC have fallen a little bit behind in League, while no definitive harm has been inflicted. It might be concluded that the team and squad have coped well without Suarez.

When it comes to the level of play showed, though, my personal impression is that Suarez has been sorely missed. In Carling Cup, the first leg of the semi-final started with what was probably the best performance of the team for quite a while. Really a joy to watch. Regrettably, it only lasted for about 20/25 minutes. From then on, the team sat back and simply rejected to even try to play. Wise movement, may be argued seeing the result. But I think that the defence was not particularly good in that game, and only that many a time elusive Lady Luck accounted for the clean sheet and the win. The second leg was far better on the whole game, and the team really deserved to go through.

In FA Cup, the 5-1 win against Oldham was a deserved win, but 2-1, or 3-1, would have reflected better what happened. In the first half the team really struggled, and was probably inferior. They reacted well in second half, and ran out comfortable winners. In the following round, 2-1 victory against ManU was nothing more than the team deserved. It was not a brilliant game, but ManU hardly troubled Reina while the team that showed real will to win was undoubtedly LFC. I would like to highlight the almost clairvoyance of the substitutions by Dalglish. I confess I am not a great fan of his substitution policy, but on this game he was spot on.

Turning to league games, the 3-0 defeat against Man City was a hard outcome, but overall LFC were second best on that night, and never looked really challenging. Draw against Stoke was a poor performance by the team. And, as Dalglish pointed out, 3-1 defeat against Bolton was a very low point. The team did not play, and did not show the fighting spirit that should be demanded. 3-0 win against Wolves was clearly a good result, but the game was overall far from perfect. The team showed certain ambition during first half, but did not play very well; after finding the first goal, the players started to play extremely poorly. However, they scored the second goal, and from that moment they gave a professional account of themselves, clearly dominating the rest of the game, although without brilliance.

All in all, what we have seen is a team with a very, very solid defence, even in bad games. I doubt Reina has ever had a more boring month. At the other end of the pitch, however, the team is struggling. The return of Suarez will be very helpful, if he can find his form right away. It might take some games for him to hit his top form, but he will be key if the season is going to end in a high. In his absence, Bellamy has been a fantastic replacement. He has been playing extremely well, and I hope they both can play together and do no end of harm to opposition defences.

I am still unconvinced about the midfield. The area in which most efforts were done in the summer transfer window, but still failing to really deliver. Adam, Henderson and Downing have given some samples of their quality here and there, but not on a regular basis. "Old" boys like Gerrard and Spearing have been more useful players, and while Kuyt appears to have found his goalscoring form in last games, Maxi seems to have lost his.

Eight games later LFC are, hence, more or less at the same point regarding the level of play and League table, and clearly more advanced in Cup competitions. And Bellamy has revealed himself as the bargain of the season. By any means, Suarez can help to give the team the extra push needed to step up its level.

30.- A spell cast on the opposite goal

Date: 3-February-2012
Previous results: Tottenham U19 1-0 LFC U19 (NextGen Series)

Sometimes football matches escape all logic, all analysis, and one is heavily tempted to resort to spells, witches, gnomes, and the like, in trying to explain the outcome of a match, given what happened on the pitch. For me, one such game was Tottenham-LFC in U19 tournament NextGen Series, Wednesday night. Not only during the match, but also after it had finished.

To clarify, I am not referring here to that more or less frequent matches in which a certain sense of injustice prevails at the end. Rather, I am thinking in those matches in which it seems almost supernatural that certain team cannot score, no matter what. The balls go to the woodwork, inches out of goalposts, rebound in defenders, or even in other strikers,...

Something of the like happened in that NextGen Series match. After a cautious and pretty uneventful beginning by both teams, LFC started to grab the match, and, little by little, take it to Tottenham half. Not that the match was one way. Tottenham are also a very good team with great and promising players. But LFC looked during almost the whole match the most likely to score.

However, chances were being squandered time and again. Not many, but very clear ones, whereas Tottenham kept the ball at a times, but without really threatening to get a goal. Things were going more or less the same way in the second half when, with about 20 minutes remaining, Tottenham were able to capitalise on a bad rebound on a LFC defender, and a not totally accurate goalkeeping by Bedford, and got the opener.

Up until that moment, one could simply talk about a case of severe bad luck, and a goal against the run of the game. But the remaining of the game, with LFC trying to get the equaliser and Tottenham restricted to their own half, when not to their own box, was more and more difficult to believe.

All sorts of balls went to the box, and directed at Tottenham goal, which started to seem enchanted. No way a ball would go inside. And, while the keeper did well, most of the chances were not really stopped by him, the ball looking as having a distinct will of not going into the goal. Exactly as if a spell had been cast on that goal to remain closed.

It was as if either Jonathan Strange or Mister Norrell (or both) were Tottenham fans. (I highly recommend the novel by Susanna Clarke to those of you who have not read it; nothing to do with football, much to do with magic). However, once the game had finished, the magicians turned out to be LFC fans, given the withdrawal of Tottenham that will mean the qualification of LFC for the semi-finals.

I guess almost any football fan can remember al least a handful of those games, in which the ball simply refuses to get into the goal. I have recently seen the highlights of an England-Italy match from 1973 which falls into this category, while one the best examples is another England match played also in Wembley the same year, that England-Poland (which admittedly involved an out of this world performance by the Polish goalkeeper and ended 1-1, so England managed to score once, albeit with a penalty; but England had a total of 35 shots at goal) that meant England was going to miss the World Cup the following year.

I can also remember a game in the Spanish league, 2003/04 season, in which Real Madrid were clearly outplayed by Athletic Bilbao, but ran out 3-0 winners thanks to the same kind of magic that prevented Athletic from scoring, no matter what they did or tried. Or a match between Barcelona and Sevilla this 2011/2012 season that ended 0-0, the final action of the match being a penalty mistake by none other than Messi.

Even the Clubs World Cup final of 2005 between LFC and Sao Paulo might be put in this category, after LFC failed to get a goal in a number of chances while Sao Paulo scored in almost its only attempt. Not to forget, though, that previously to that match LFC had a string of nearly ten matches without conceding a single goal. However, I would attribute that to the tactical acumen by Benitez and the quality of the players rather than to the kind of magic I am writing about.

Obviously, I am not for one moment suggesting that the only analysis of the U19 game, and U19 team, is that some magic prevented the team from winning. Once the competition should have finished for LFC, had it not been for the Tottenham withdraw, it is time to assess the performance. I tend to think that the team have done just OK, until now; the new line of live might be a good chance to improve that impression of probably having underachieved a bit on the whole competition. In group stage, the team was very inferior to Sporting Lisbon, superior to Molde, and just about the level of Wolfsburg. I think a little bit more could have been expected from them. And now they have the chance to live up to those expectations.

Against Tottenham, both full backs (McLaughlin and Flanagan) suffered at a times, and Flanagan, playing on the left, could not help the attack as much as he usually does on the right. Central defenders (Wisdom and Sama) did OK, though the goal might have been avoidable at some point. Central midfielders (Coady and Roddan) were at their usual great level in the defensive and physical side, but some flair and creativity are being missed on that area.

However, the best and to some extent worse news were found in the attacking four. I can hardly think of a more exciting quartet of U19 LFC players than Silva and Sterling on the flanks, Suso on the hole and Ngoo up front. And indeed they produced some fantastic football. Silva was a little bit lost against Tottenham, and Suso performed some really great actions, though one is always left wanting more from him.

Sterling was by far the man of the match. That was the match of a player that wants first team action, and wants it now. He is probably not fully ready now, but I have a feeling that I am not the only one who would like to see him given some minutes. He is quick, lively, can manage the ball, can pass players. He lacks certain accuracy in his passes and his shots at goal, and need to learn to choose better options.

And I must confess that I don't know what to make of Ngoo. He seems unplayable at times: tall, strong, skilful,...while at the same time he can look clumsy the following moment, and unable to handle the ball. I will need to see him play more times to reach a conclusion. What seems clear, though, even in his best moments, is that he has troubles with scoring. If anything else, he definitely needs to work on that.

After all, if the better strikers have usually problems with scoring and turning the chances into goals, it is maybe unnecessary to resort to magic to explain the lack of goals. Anyway, some matches look supernatural, some goals look enchanted, at times, don't they?

31.- Ability and will

Date: 8-February-2012
Previous results: LFC 0-0 Tottenham (Premier League)

Very often a football match conveys not only joy and frustration, emotion and anger, but also more vague sensations, feelings, ideas. The match between LFC and Tottenham illustrated, at least in my case, some of these feelings you get by watching a football match.

What I saw was a confrontation between two ways of facing football; on one side there was a team with a tremendous will to do everything within its power to win the match, but that in that particular moment lacked the ability to achieve it; on the other side a team we all know has the potential, the ability, to develop an ambitious play, but that lacked the will to go and really try to win the match.

LFC were obviously the first case. The team always fought, always tried, but somehow the ability was not there. Probably the string of three games in Man City, ManU, and Wolves drained to a certain extent the stamina, or the football brain, of the players. What was missing, in my view, was not the desire, not the sheer class, but the capacity to drag from inside themselves all the ability that the players have, and put it on the pitch. They seemed a bit tired, psychologically. They wanted, but weren't able to show all their football strength.

Tottenham were the second case. Judging by their performances, they probably would have taken the 0-0 draw without playing, if possible. They simply waited for the match to finish, and showed not really wish, nor will, to really play the match, or show their ability. An ability we the football fans know that was there, but that there was nowhere to be seen during the match.

Hence, we had this contest between will and ability. A contest that ended in a draw. LFC had more chances, but Tottenham had the best one, in that one-one that confronted Bale and Reina. LFC could claim his "right" to win on the grounds of its far superior ambition, that lead to the game being played mostly on Tottenham half and the ball possession being mostly LFC's. But, to be fair, that elusive first goal never seemed like coming, there were very few clear-cut chances, and this time nobody has said anything about the performance of the rival goalkeeper.

Once again, it was commendable the solidity of the team structure. Only once Tottenham were able to break it (that one-on-one mentioned above), and if LFC goal was never likely, Tottenham goal looked almost an impossibility. That defensive solidity has been achieved with an unlikely (for me) central pair of Agger and Skrtel.

Agger is a top-class centre-defender, no doubt about that. And being able to play week in, week out is doing him no end of good. Should he remain injury free he might become the cornerstone of LFC defence for years to come. Skrtel is much weaker, in my view. I would have bet a Carragher-Agger pair would be more effective. But until now, and for many matches, Agger-Skrtel has delivered well enough.

The flanks needed a change this time, with Johnson on the left and Kelly on the right. Both worked well. Still, Johnson loses a great deal of his effectiveness on the left flank, and Kelly probably, and understandably, still lacks a little bit of the confidence that only matches will provide. But he did well, supported the attack at times, and was never put in trouble in defence.

Team solidity, however, is a matter of the team as a whole, not only defenders. And Spearing helped a lot, both stopping the odd attack by Tottenham and directing the beginning of LFC attacks. He had a very good game overall, only marred by some strange mistakes in clear passes. Adam did his work on the pitch, but was not able to really stamp his authority on the match, nor provide the losing link between midfield and the final third.

Gerrard produced some outstanding football, probably the best pieces of football craft seen in the night, but was very irregular on his appearances, maybe lacking the rhythm of matches after his injuries. Still, indispensable player for the team. On the wings, Kuyt and Bellamy could not find the way to pass the Tottenham defenders and create chances in the box. Bellamy was below his high standard of this season, but never lacked work, run, ambition,…he probably epitomised LFC match more than anyone: desire without inspiration, work without reward.

As a striker, Carroll certainly worked his socks off. He showed a mobility that in many matches would have caused the opposition defenders all sorts of problems. He fought, and often gained, some aerial battles, but, either because lack of luck, or because good defending by Tottenham, there were not clear benefits from his work.

The entry of Suarez was like a breeze of fresh air all over the team. As Dalglish said, you have always the impression that something is going to happen the moment the ball is close to him. But it was difficult to break the defence, and finally the team took only a draw for all its efforts.

Even so, the players were more than willing to try until the end, did not accept the draw until the final whistle, and showed a remarkable amount of ambition. But what they did not show in this match was the necessary edge, quality, ability, to overcome a stern defence. Hence, two more points vanished, and doubts over the potential of the squad to become title contenders remained.

In this particular game, LFC failed, and Tottenham obtained what they were looking for. Having said that, of the two teams on the pitch, I would happily take LFC desire and will to win over Tottenham hidden ability and presumed class. And I would happily take this performance by LFC, frustrating as the result was, over that second half against Man City in the league cup that ended in a narrow victory. I prefer my team to fight the matches and show their strengths rather than try to nullify the opposition at the price of nullifying themselves at the same time.

When it comes to football, much as I would like to support a team with plenty of will, and plenty of ability, I would always pick will over ability if forced to choose.

P.S.: after writing this entry, I read about the sad death of Jessie Paisley. My condolences to her family and friends. YNWA.

32.- Performance marking

Date: 16-February-2012
Previous results: ManUnited 2-1 LFC (Premier League)

When trying to mark the quality (or lack of it) of a football team performance we usually struggle. How to encapsulate in a single digit the nuances of a given display? Is it even possible? Well, I don't think it is really possible, maybe it isn't helpful. But sometimes there is a match that provides us with that chance. Something of the like happened in the ManU match last weekend.

The difference between this match and most of the rest, in that sense, is that LFC performed excellently well during a brief spell in the game, and awfully badly in the rest of it. So one can try and mark that performance in that way: LFC entered the game brilliantly, and kept that level for about 10 minutes. Then, abruptly, started to play weakly until the last 5 minutes, in which a draw was almost achieved.

Thus, about 15 good minutes and 75 very poor, which amount for 1/6 of maximum grade, or between 15% and 20%. Let's make it 20%, even 25% if you want, given that not every minute of those 75 was totally unacceptable, and there were certain good actions, especially in the defensive side of game.

However, only in one aspect of defence. In football there are two different tasks when the opposite team is in possession: on the one hand, the first concern is not conceding a goal against; on the other hand, the team needs to try and get the ball back. LFC have been excelling in the first one for several weeks, now. And in ManU game, too. Other than the goals, ManU had little to show for all their dominance of the match, in terms of goal chances.

That is clearly a good trait in a football team, and something that Dalglish and Clarke (and probably other members of the staff) can rightly claim as a success. But regarding the other task, things are way less promising. And that is something I found very discouraging about that match: that during long spells, well into the second half, the team looked more like trying to avoid more goals against than trying to get back into the game. A kind of attitude that would have made it impossible that 3-3 against Milan in Istanbul. There were apparently no hungry to get the ball back, to chase the ManU players, who passed the ball comfortably to each other while LFC players looked apathetic, disengaged. It was almost like going back to the Bolton game; but there have been no similar reactions between the players and technical staff. One can almost get a sense of acceptance that there was no way LFC could get anything from Old Trafford.

In a way, all of these goes back to what could be seen on the Tottenham game at Anfield; the players try to do the right things, the things they are expected to perform, but in a "flat" way. They seem unconfident on themselves, as if there is nothing they can do to change course, as if they accepted the situation. Probably things would have been different if during those first ten minutes LFC would have scored. When they have something to defend, the players look distinctly focus and uncompromising. That happened in both legs in League Cup semi-final, and that happened in the FA Cup match against ManU.

But once they fall behind, or they spend too much time without achieving, it is like a shadow fell on the players. And then, when final whistle approaches, they get energized again, and normally end the games well into the opposition half, if not opposition box. Only that, many a time, it is a case of too little too late, either for getting the equalizer at Old Trafford, or the winning goal at Anfield in those recurrent draws.

It is something that can be seen not only in the defensive side of the game, but also in the offensive side. When in possession, LFC look normally flat, dull, without ideas. The players take the ball, pass it to a team-mate, and wait for the ball to eventually come back. Of the Shankly Holy Trinity of "take, give, move", that "move" has been sorely missed in last games.

Not that the quality is not there; during those spells at the beginning of matches, and sometimes at the end of them, the play is often fluid, and goal chances are coming the LFC way. But there is a persistent lack of consistency, and good runs of play seldom last for more than 15/20 minutes.

At some point, players seem to lose confidence and start to play in a very automatic way, which is more or less good enough to avoid goals against, but is not good enough to defend actively, or to attack effectively. When going in the attack, one (not the only) key is mobility, position changes, runs in and out the box, full backs and midfielders appearing in unexpected zones, strikers dropping to midfield areas to clear spaces,...It is about creating uncertainties in the opposition.

Almost nothing of these is to be seen in all those "flat" spells of games. Against ManU, during the first ten minutes, you could see plenty of LFC players in opposition half, supporting each other, and making themselves available. Once the match entered in the bad (for LFC) moments of play, hardly three, maybe four, players would get in the other half, even when in possession. The man with the ball had almost no choice, other than try a long ball and pray for Suarez to get to it.

Which is not a fitting way to attack any team, let alone ManU at Old Trafford. Meanwhile, Carrick, Scholes and Giggs would hang onto the ball for as much time as they liked, passing it along. It is amazing that three players their age could overcome Spearing, Gerrard, Henderson with such easiness. And things were not much better (although admittedly they were slightly better) with Adam or Bellamy on the pitch.

All in all, a very disappointing match, with a few promising signs. Flat and plain as the team looked, it did never collapse, and the basic structure remained solid during the match. As a result, the score was never decided. Indeed, that last shot by Johnson could have earned the team a draw. It is a good sign that the team is able to keep the result within reach even in a poorly played game. And there are the huge positives from the first minutes of the match, which showed the way along which the team should keep working. During those minutes, the team were really, really, good.

So a very poor display, combined with some bright signs and some hope for a near future improvement. I would stick to my 25% mark, really hoping that the team keeps working and that mark would end up being far better than that.

33.- Young derbies, youth system

Date: 22-February-2012
Previous results: LFC 6-1 Brighton (FA Cup); LFC Reserves 1-1 Everton Reserves

LFC vs Everton is always a significant event in Merseyside, even if at youth level. This week we have two of those matches, reserves on Tuesday and U18 on Friday. And those two games against Everton in a short period of time have prompted me to share some views on English youth developing system. I know that reserves teams don't have age limits. And, admittedly, David Weir starting for Everton undermines my point. But, generally speaking, reserves teams can be seen as part of that system.

Which I think poses a big challenge to the clubs. I have said elsewhere that fixtures at youth level are a big problem in England. The problem increases as the players approach the first team, particularly from U18s level, and it becomes almost dramatic with players more than 18 years of age. The fixtures are annoyingly irregular, with weeks, even months, without a competitive game, and weeks with more than one game. That severely impedes the proper formation of players.

Up until 18 years, a big part of the formation lies on proper training, with competitive matches merely complementing the process, so the players can, to a certain extent, develop their qualities and correct their weaknesses within the club and the current system. At U18 level the proper competition quickly becomes an integral part of the formation process, and the English system begins to fail to achieve the main goal of making the most of players' capabilities.

The problem is much bigger after 18 years. The players are considered senior players right away. But very few of them are ready for Premier League football. Of course, it is not a big problem for the Gerrards, the Fowlers, the Owens, the Carraghers,…they have scarcely played for the reserves, and shortly after (or even before) their 18th birthday they were promoted to the first team.

But, for the great majority of players the period between 18 and, say, 21 years of age can be decisive, can decide whether a player would make it to the first level football or remain a merely good player outside the top level. That is a step in which the scarcity, irregularity, and lack of competitiveness in reserves league games can really ruin careers.

There are obviously ways to solve it. To begin with, many Premier League clubs have very few, or even none at all, club grown players. They simply sign players from other clubs, in and out England, when needed. The academies nurture players but knowing that they will almost surely end up in lower leagues. There is also the "Arsenal way", accelerate the promotion of the players to the first team, at the risk of stopping their formation too soon, thus preventing them from developing their full potential.

Much more successful seems to be the "ManU way", loaning players to Premier League teams for full seasons to finalise their preparation for first team duties. Cleverley, Welbeck, are current examples. If the players prove not to be good enough, they have at least been tested, and can be transferred or released knowing that they didn't have the proper level.

The "Liverpool FC way" in this respect seems to be to loan the players to lower division teams, usually for short periods of time. On the plus side, they experience full competitive games, and meaningful matches, which add to their baggage. On the minus side, they seldom become really members of a team, due to the short spells spent there, and they confront opposition way below Premier League standard. Plus, they lose also their belonging to LFC reserves for being in and out.

I am not convinced of this strategy and its usefulness to properly end the formation of the players. To name just a few cases: Danny Guthrie is now a Newcastle player, with good performances in the Premier League. I agree that he is not, as of now, an LFC-level player, but could he have become a useful squad member should he have had another path after reserves level? Not that I have the answer; I don't know, but maybe. Neil Mellor was a very promising striker at LFC Academy, he had some glory moments in first team (Olympiakos, Arsenal), but maybe, just maybe, he would have become a better player with a loan to a Premier League team. Adam Hammill was once a hot LFC Academy prospect, and is now struggling to make the team in Wolves. I still wonder if he could have become a much better player had it not been for that quick succession of loan spells with lower league teams in key years for making the grade.

There are many more examples, and the reality is that we will never know what might have happened in another circumstances. But the strategy of short loans to lower leagues teams is not working well. I think the scheme needs to be rethought and eventually modified. As seen this week against Everton, there is one player who will need proper assessment in the very near future. LFC technical staff has to decide if Eccleston has in it what it takes to make first team squad.

He has turned 21, and has had three loan spells. It makes little sense to keep him in the reserves team next season. Next summer, he should either be promoted, or loaned for the whole season to another Premier League (or overseas) team in which he could have the playing time he needs. I think he should be promoted; he would have been probably of better use to the squad than, say, Downing, this season. Anyway, he is not a reserves team player. He is head and shoulders above the rest of them, as seen, also but not only, in the Sterling goal against Everton. A clear path to first level football should be offered to him. The risk is for him not to fulfil his potential. Or, even worse, not to ever know his full potential. I must add, to be fair, that I have full confidence in Borrell to assess the situation. In fact, I have much more confidence in him than in me, in that respect.

More generally, English football as a whole needs to think about this issue. I tend to favour a scheme in which the clubs are allowed to have squads in the lower leagues. Thus, the young players can stay in their clubs, and the clubs are able to have a close eye on them. But, at the same time, they can experience full competitive football, and a proper schedule of matches. Not to forget that the players can remain under the guidance of club coaches, that are able to combine the needs of the competition with those of educating the players.

It is not a perfect system, and can also have its flaws, and setbacks. Having said that, I think that some kind of action needs to be taken regarding the last and key steps in the formation of players in England.

In the meantime, we all can keep enjoying the young derbies, so to speak. 1-1 in the first one (this week), on Friday we will have the second. And this derby week could have been complete: had it not been for LFC reaching the Carling Cup final, a senior derby would have closed the week on weekend. But I could do without a derby during the weekend if LFC can win a trophy at Wembley.

34.- Winning titles, playing football

Date: 28-February-2012
Previous results: LFC 2-2 Cardiff, 3-2 on penalty shoot-out (Carling Cup final)

Almost six years without any titles are many years for a club the size of LFC's. Fortunately, that gap ended last Sunday with the Carling Cup, and the first title won in the new Wembley. Not the only statistic gap filled: Dalglish became only the seventh manager to win all three major titles in English football. Having won also the Community Shield, he has no voids to fill in his list of local accolades. Not to mention he also won all of them as a player, meaning he has nothing new to aspire to in English football.

Luckily, as we all have heard these days, achieving successes not only does not have the effect of calming the thirst for titles, but has the contrary effect of stimulating the desire to keep on enjoying finals and adding pieces of silverware to the records, both individual for players and managers and collective for the clubs. So it is a safe bet that not only has Dalglish even more ambition than before completing his list of trophies, but also the players will be raring to go and return to Wembley and winning ways as soon as possible.

This has happened before and will happen again. The momentum, the winning habit, can help raise the level of a team, turning a bad team into a mediocre one, a mediocre one into a good one, and a good one into a really great team. However, it is not automatic, obviously. The mechanism is not "you win a title and from then you keep on winning". Ask Birmingham after their Carling Cup title last year.

The effects of winning a title are boosting the confidence of the team as a whole and of the players, increase the feel-good factor in the team, and ultimately improve the level of play. Hence, the subsequent titles. Without improving the quality of play there is not a promise of keeping adding titles. Winning a title stands a team in good stead from that moment on. It is up to the players and technical staff to capitalise on that and effectively raise the level of the team.

That is the challenge ahead for Dalglish and the squad. Being able to reproduce the kind of winning trend that in 2001 led the team from the League Cup to the UEFA Cup, the FA Cup and, last but not the least, qualification for the Champions League. And, hopefully, keep on the momentum to become a team really capable of competing for the Premier League. That 2001 team were far from being the finalised product. So is the 2012 team. But both, 2001's and 2012's, were (and are) teams capable of challenging any other team on a good day. And both teams had (and have) in them the potential to provide the structure for a Premier winning team.

Houllier failed with the fine tuning of his team, and, two years later, the 2003 Carling Cup was not the beginning, but the end, of a possible great team. Benitez came very, very close to completing his rebuilding of the team, and after 2005 Champions League, 2006 FA Cup, and 2007 Champions League final, his 2008/2009 team was not only capable of challenging for the Premier League (as was

Houllier's 2001/2002 team), but in fact a team that deserved to win the League; that was the better team that season.

Sadly, out of the pitch problems prevented that squad from taking the final step. So there are, broadly speaking, two great challenges ahead: firstly, take the momentum going into the end of the season and came back to Wembley and get the fourth spot; then, make the necessary adjustments to the team in the summer so that next season the squad is better equipped to even greater challenges. As Dalglish says time and again, the task is to get the club steadily going forward.

There is indeed room for improvement. Satisfactory as it is to win a title, there is no denying the performance in the final was not even close to brilliant. As so many times this season, the team struggled severely to break down a composed defence. LFC dominated the match in almost every moment; but, chances-wise, the match was not greatly unbalanced. Cardiff not only scored as many goals as LFC did, Cardiff created as many clear chances as LFC did. During long spells, LFC's only path to scoring was crossing balls into the box from set pieces. And LFC defence looked somewhat less solid than in previous matches.

Even so, LFC were deserved winners, no doubt about that. They were the better team, the players endlessly pursued the victory, they took the game to Cardiff half. But, much as we have heard these days that finals are not played, only won and lost, the truth is that, in the long term, the better you play, the better results you get. And, with Arsenal waiting in the weekend, the level of play does matter.

And that level needs to be raised if the season is to end up in a high. On the defensive side, the injury to Agger is bad news, and Van Persie will test soon enough the capacity of LFC to keep up its up to now good defensive displays. On the midfield front, Gerrard is still trying to adjust his game to a holding role, and is not having on the games the impact usually expected, while Adam is not playing as the playmaker the team needs. As for the attack, both in the wings and in the centre the team needs to create more troubles, and ask more questions, to opposition defences.

The reassuring side is that LFC have consistently proved its ability to deliver against the better teams, so it can be expected a much needed good performance against Arsenal. A defeat would make it extremely difficult to achieve fourth spot, so Saturday match is, in a sense, a new final. And something LFC can do, and do well, is perform well in finals. In a final you need playing qualities, but you also need determination, will, not acceptance of defeat, mental strength, drive, fighting spirit.

LFC have, time and again, proved along the years its capacity to play and win finals, either through outplaying the rivals, or through sheer will. 2012 Carling Cup was won on penalties, after arguably the two most reliable LFC players on that front failed their shoots. Too bad league games are not decided on penalties. I bet most of those costing eight draws at Anfield would have been turned into victories.

One title already in Anfield, the team needs now to take the impetus and go on a winning run, starting next Saturday. In order to do that, determination and mental strength will be needed. But also an improved level of play, a better way to break down the opposition through footballing skills like passes, crosses, movements, and goals. In the end, playing good football is the best way to adding points to Premier league table. And, while far from perfect, this LFC team and LFC players have in them the ability to keep improving and play better football. The Carling Cup could help and provide them with the confidence to take that extra step.

35.- Some disconnected thoughts

Date: 8-March-2012
Previous results: Everton Reserves 0-0 LFC Reserves; LFC 1-2 Arsenal (Premier League)

Last match against Arsenal has left many comments to make, issues to deal with, ideas to discuss. I just wanted to share some points with fellow LFC fans:

1) Probably the race for fourth spot is now over, but the League is not. It might be now, more than ever, the moment to test that idea that has become almost part of LFC DNA: one match at a time, add the points at the end of season, and see where it places the club in the table. Admittedly, I am one of those fans that like to scrutinize the fixtures, calculate the points expected, compare with the points tally of other seasons,…but there is no point now in targeting Arsenal. There is much point, though, in playing the best football the team is able to, winning as much points as they can, and look at the table again in four, five, matches, to see where they are. Fourth spot might seem as unreachable then as it seems to be now; or maybe things have developed well, and it is not impossible. Either way, the team needs desperately to improve its league form, which implies to find the way to sustain a winning form for several matches, not being so unpredictable, with some good matches followed by really bad performances, and vice versa.

2) Final League position matters, even out of the top four. Some may think that, once the team is in the Europa League

via the Carling Cup, it doesn't really matter whether the final position is 5th, 6th, or even 9th or 10th. But, for both sets of fans, "pragmatic" and "idealistic", final position does matter. For the pragmatists, the higher the team ends in the League, the later round it enters the Europa League. It might make a lot of difference in pre-season, having to play from the end of July, or entering the competition way into August. Even if that were not the case, LFC should try to finish as high in the League as possible, always. I am well aware that, according to Shankly, "If you are first, you are first. If you are second, you are nothing"; let alone if you are, say, 6th. But I am not convinced. LFC should try to get as many points as possible, and end up in the table as higher as they can.

3) Regularity is a top target. The team needs to find a way to, on the one hand, get much better results against "lesser" teams, particularly (although not only) at Anfield, and, on the other hand, achieve a certain grade of reliability. It is very well to compete well against the better teams, to perform well in Cup competitions, to give the occasional glimpse of greatness. But what the team has been lacking for much time, now, is that reliability; and I cannot see signs of it improving. As a fan, I don't know what I will find when a match starts.

4) The accuracy in front of goal must be dramatically improved. It is about time all of us, including those inside the club, stopped talking about "luck". While undoubtedly a factor, even a key factor, there should surely be other aspects in it. When shooting from distance, LFC players usually perform the shoots very poorly, resulting, very often, in the ball well over the bar. When shooting from inside the

box, they find it difficult to find the angles of the goal, finding the goal-keeper or the woodwork much more often. Particularly, I think it is telling the level of difficulties experienced this season with the penalties, normally a strong point for LFC. During 2011/12 season, Suarez, Kuyt, Carroll, and Adam have missed a combined total of six penalties. That is a huge amount, both of penalties missed and of number of different players involved. Obviously there is no way of replicating the pressure of a real match in training pitch; but I suppose something can be done; in fact, I am pretty sure something is being done on that front. The moment the footballs start getting regularly into the opposition goal, it will be a huge boost for the confidence of the players, thus improving in turn the level of play…and the number of goals scored.

5) Incidentally, a similar problem seems to be tormenting the reserves team. Probably, unrelated issue. But a striking coincidence, all the same. It seemed almost unbelievable that the match against Everton on Tuesday ended with a "0" in LFC score. Admittedly, Everton could have scored, too, avoiding that final 0-0. But it was LFC which had more, and clearer, chances.

6) Arsenal game is a good platform to build on. There is a long debate that has gone on for decades, and will as likely as not continue for ever, about the hypothetical choice between "playing well" and "winning". I firmly stand with the idea that, in the long term, playing well is the better way to win. There are obviously many ways of playing well, and endless football conversations on that. I think that against Arsenal, LFC played very well. In fact, they played nearly as well as this team is capable of. The team was positive in its

approach, went for the match, outplayed Arsenal for most of the game, created more than enough clear chances to win, conceded very few chances to Arsenal. And, overall, more than deserved to win. Many positives could be taken from that match. The way in which Suarez and Kuyt absolutely tormented Arsenal defenders, with all their mobility, their search for spaces, the linking with the midfielders, can be of use in future matches. The almost free role that, now and then, took Henderson during the match, combined with some spells on the right, seemed to show his better version. Spearing showed again that he can provide the midfield with much needed consistency.

I think that a very good team can be built on that performance, adjusting details, polishing imperfections, and reinforcing the weakest positions. In that sense, the Arsenal game, disappointing as it was in its result, may have given an indication of some lines in which the squad may work, may keep working.

But the first step is, in my view, the consistency, the reliability. Against Sunderland, I hope to see a similar performance; I hope to see a team with a recognisable playing identity.

36.- Luck and lessons to learn

Date: 15-March-2012
Previous results: Sunderland 1-0 LFC (Premier League); LFC 3-0 Everton (Premier League); LFC U19 0-6 Ajax U19 (NextGen Series)

A quick succession in matches during last days have provided with some insight about football and some valuable lessons. I would like, first of all, to reflect on that elusive, yet ever-present, factor in football: Lady Luck. I fully acknowledge the idea that "luck" has a part to play in football, and that sometimes developments can be explained through good, or bad, luck.

But on occasions the resort to "luck" is unjustified, and only serves to hide the real facts. I am thinking, for example, in Bendtner goal for Sunderland against LFC. I don't think it was "bad luck". In fact, normally a ball hitting twice the woodwork would have been considered as good, rather than bad, luck for LFC. Moreover, the moment Campbell shoots, Coates is closer to Reina's goal than Bendtner; Bendtner's advantage was the inertia of him already running, but if Bendtner gets to the ball not only before Coates, but in fact with acres of space, that is not bad luck; that is bad defending.

So, was the defeat Coates' fault? Not in the slightest, I reckon. He could certainly have played better, but it was a really poor performance for the team as a whole. Again. In the mould of that at Bolton. LFC never looked like scoring, like winning the game, like dominating at all. Steve Gerrard has been much more realistic in his words about the game than Dalglish. It was a very discouraging display, very worrying for the fans. The team looks, time and again, incapable of raising its level against "lesser" teams. Not only the results, but also (and mainly) the level of play. That happened with Houllier, with Benitez, with Hodgson, with Dalglish. That is not bad luck; that is something else. And something that needs to be sorted out.

Neither was it bad luck the penalty missed by Suso in the U19 heavy defeat against Ajax. For those not familiar with the match, Ajax went ahead in the first minutes of the match, and a few minutes later a penalty was awarded to LFC. So 1-1 looked as coming. If the regular penalty taker, Coady, would have taken it, and missed, that might, just might, had been bad luck. But if, after some arguments on the pitch, it is Suso who takes the penalty, maybe (I am not totally sure) his first of the season in a competitive game, and misses it, that is not bad luck; it is poor decision. Again, this is not to say Suso is in anyway to be blamed for the 6-0 defeat. But it is not realistic to think that the penalty was missed due to bad luck, once the team opted for a new shooter.

However, the most alleged "bad luck" this season has been that of the many squandered goal chances. I fully accept that, to a certain extent, bad luck is a major factor in that. But not the only factor. Gerrard gave a magnificent course of finishing and goal-scoring during the 3-0 against Everton. First, with his "bad" foot, he sweetly put the ball on the net; that was not a shot; that was a pass to the net. That was great. Then, he splashed the ball into the net for his second on the night, making it impossible for any defender to stop the ball. Finally, he didn't simply stare at Suarez after passing the ball to him; he accompanied the action, looked for space, and made himself available. The rest was the unselfishness by Suarez. None of those actions were good luck; they were good footballing.

A lesson that should be learnt. Another lesson was taught by U19 Ajax players. Simply a joy to watch how the strikers, when in position to shot at goal, aimed at the corners time and again, leaving the goalkeeper helpless. At so early an age, those players were able to repeatedly put their chances away, finding the net ruthlessly. LFC U19 players mirrored their seniors in being unable to get pass the goalkeeper. They only found the inside of the opposition goal when they found the goalkeeper. If not, the ball went wide, or high. Surely bad luck to a point; as surely, bad shooting technique also. Something the U19s, but also the senior LFC players, can learn.

Borrell said that this was his worst day in sport. Not surprising, given the 6-0 defeat. But hopefully the players are clever enough to learn from the match, and become better players. They need to keep calm in front of goal, thus improving their conversion rate. But they also need to keep their focus. After the penalty missed, each time LFC players found themselves in possession inside the Ajax box (and in the first time there were several occasions), they seemed to be thinking more on getting another penalty than on scoring a goal; they mistook the referee as their opponent, instead of the opposition team. That often happens even to senior players, but it should be avoided. Proper focus is key to success in almost every field in life; and surely it is in football.

Another good lesson would be to make the most of the footballing qualities. This is clearly a vague statement. But I don't think that every Ajax player is better than every LFC player. What I do think is that Ajax players knew how to bank on their qualities, and how to maintain their focus during the game. LFC players were able to some really brilliant actions, but failed to take advantage of them. Overall, they probably need more matches against really strong teams. In that sense, this season on the NextGen Series could do the world of good to the players; if that happens, the 6-0 defeat would have been worth taking.

There have been lessons for the first team, too. Sunderland match made it crystal clear than intensity, ambition, desire, hunger,...are irreplaceable for a winning team. They are not substitutes for real quality, technique, or class; but they are needed. This is not something new, I am sure every LFC player and fan is well aware of this. But it is proving to be a very hard lesson to learn. Surely the players want to be ambitious, and focused; but they find it difficult to show it on the pitch, especially on away matches.

And the derby match showed another irreplaceable piece of the team. Spearing is, as of now, with this squad, a key player. He provides consistency, solidity, circulation of the ball,...and the opportunity for Gerrard to appear on the opposition box, causing havoc on the opponents and not holes on the LFC midfield. To become a really first class player, a really LFC-level player, Spearing needs to keep growing. As of now, he is very valuable but not a top class player. But, as of now, he is key to LFC midfield. Hopefully he can keep on progressing and growing as a player.

Reflections on the part that luck plays in football, several lessons, some disappointments and a great result, youngsters and seniors,…and eventful week for LFC.

37.- Creative anger

Date: 22-March-2012
Previous results: LFC 2-1 Stoke (FA Cup); WBA 3-2 LFC (Premier League)

According to Bruce Springsteen, in rock and roll you can not go wrong if you are angry. I don't know if the same applies to football writing. But I am certainly angry (don't get me wrong; I am speaking only football wise) as I write, after what happened against QPR last night.

There was no way that match should be lost, 2-0 up at 75th minute against a very troubled and demoralised team, having been far superior until that moment. Keep playing the same, keeping control of the game, was about everything that was needed to end the match, collect the three points, and keep the league season alive and kicking.

But somehow the team managed to allow three goals in Reina's goal in last 15 minutes, hence losing the game. Was there a certain dose of bad luck in that? Most likely; even being totally outplayed, a team is unlikely to be 3 goals down after 15/20 minutes. Take, for example, the first minutes of the same match, in which LFC in fact absolutely outplayed, destroyed, QPR, with no goals scored. And LFC were not by any means outplayed in those final 20 minutes. In fact, QPR looked perfectly harmless even during those last minutes. Harmless, that is, except for the appalling defending of the crosses, and the last long ball.

So, yes, to a certain extent bad luck is to blame. But if the team dwells on that single explanation, there will be some lessons missed. As said, the team started the team very well, almost brilliantly at moments; but, after about 25 minutes it came to an end. The team lost their rhythm, their press, their quick recovering of the ball, and their movement when in possession, their damaging to the opposition.

After half-time, there were some glimpses of improvement, though the players were not able to come back to that previous level of play. But then it came that beauty of a goal by Coates, a terrific showing of technique, confidence and accuracy. And after Kuyt's goal in 72th minute the game looked all but decided. Sadly, LFC players thought that it was it, and stopped playing. They started defending only by keeping position and a close eye on the ball, but with no pressure, no real try of getting the ball back, simply waiting for the game to end.

Lets be honest, that would have been more than enough in almost every game; and if it was not, was because of gross mistakes by the defenders. So there are two lessons to be learnt. On the one hand, if the team would have kept their focus, impeding the QPR game from the back, the ball would have never come ever near LFC box, and the game would have been safe. On the other hand, if you opt to defend in your box, you have to do that, defend as if your life depends on it. And LFC players did not do that, they looked relaxed, overconfident. Even so, it is normally not costly; but it was this time, and luck played only a part in it.

So I ended the match angry. Overall, it was not a particularly bad game, and Reina had hardly anything to do, other than pick up three balls from inside his goal. 20/25 very good minutes, 45/50 flat, dull, but not terrible, and 15/20 in which the loss of focus cost the game, the points, and who knows what more for future games and end of league, in terms of confidence and motivation. We can only hope the team will be able to stay put and focus for the rest of the season.

Elsewhere in the week, LFC had another matches. To start with, having experienced first hand the taste of playing a cup match at Wembley, LFC players were anxious to repeat, and made sure Stoke were not going to prevent them from a new trip to London.

I wouldn't go as far as to say it was a good match; but it was a match in which LFC managed to stamp its authority, and never looked in danger of losing, or even drawing. Players were focused, limited Stoke's options, and gave a professional display. Not brilliant, but solid.

On the minus side, the amount of clear chances for LFC was very limited, and a one-goal difference is never enough to be safe. Of course, also in the minus side there is a special place for the way in the Stoke's goal was scored. Crouch is a great menace in set pieces, of course, and difficult to defend. But for him to head the ball inside the six-yard box and unmarked, directly from a corner kick, involved surely a big mistake by the defenders. Fortunately it was a goal that ultimately did not cost, but, even so, it will surely be taken as a wake-up call for set-pieces defending in following matches.

On the plus side, although not brilliant, the performance was enough to accomplish the target for the day, and accomplish it deservedly and without real threats. The defending side of the team (obviously meaning not only the defenders, but the entire defence structure), other that the mentioned Stoke's goal, seemed to have recovered its solidity, which was slightly missed after the last injury to Agger.

A solidity that remained for most of QPR game, only to vanish when it was most needed. Lot of work needs to be put in the training ground into defending the aerial balls. Stoke and QPR (twice) scored after clear mistakes than need to be avoided in future matches. Lot of work needs to be put also into making the most of the scoring chances. Some improvement could be seen during the Stoke game, in which Suarez scored a magnificent and well taken shot just in the corner of the goal. As said time and again, if a shot is well placed, it is almost impossible for the goalkeeper to save it. Too bad a similar effort could not be seen during those first minutes in QPR game, when Suarez had a one-on-one with the goalkeeper saved.

All in all, two games, similar to a point, but with very different endings. The challenge ahead is to reignite the league season, even if only to stand the team in good stead for the Cup games. Although, as I have previously written, league position matters in itself.

His rock and roll anger has led Bruce Springsteen to yet another great album, "Wrecking ball". My much more modest football anger has only led me to these thoughts shared with LFC fans all over the world. Only time will tell whether or not LFC squad have in them similar creative anger that might lead them to improving performances. I keep looking forward for the next game to get rid of the frustration.

38.- Movement, mobility

Date: 27-March-2012
Previous results: LFC 1-2 Wigan

This is being a league season really difficult to take, and to come to terms to, for LFC fans, the team seemingly fading away in last games (1 win, 1 draw, 5 defeats during February and March). What has exactly happened to the team is anyone's guess. To start with, those are not the only games played in that period, as those seven matches have been intercalated with 2 FA Cup victories and the Carling Cup final; tellingly, even taking these games into account the run of results remains poor.

I am sure a lot of work is being put, inside the club, to figure out what is happening and, more important, to improve in the very near future and getting out of this string of results that is affecting the team morale and, in that, making the players and the team look much worse than they really are.

While the team as a whole needs to improve, it is mainly the attacking side that is making the team suffer. It is very true that the injury to Agger has put into difficulties the defence, which is now struggling to keep its proper level during the complete matches. It is suffering the odd slip in concentration that in normal circumstances would not be very serious, but in last matches is being heavily penalised.

But I think the concerns should mainly go to the attacking side of the team. Analysing the final stages of the attack, eyes need to be put on the finalising, getting the ball into the net, and on the creation of chances. A lot has been spoken and written about the amount of chances squandered by LFC players this season, with the worse conversion rate in the league, the woodwork hit time and again, and the opposition goalkeepers achieving man-of-the-match displays repeatedly.

However, that is not the case in the last four or five games. Recently, it is the creation of clear-cut goal chances what is being missed. The quality of the attacking is poor, as of now; and it needs to dramatically improve if the season is going to end in a more positive note. As I see it, it is, first and foremost, movement what the players seem to lack.

One may learn by watching the best, and trying to emulate them. Other than both Manchester teams, the best attacking teams now elsewhere in Europe are Barcelona, R. Madrid, and Bayern Munich. Each of them has different approaches to scoring, with more use of the wings (Bayern), more verticality (R. Madrid), or more passes and possession (Barcelona); but they all share a group of players in constant movement, looking for and creating spaces where the opposition can be harmed.

It may, of course, be argued, that those teams are special cases, and not good examples in that they have collected some of the best players in the world. I am not sure if LFC should accept such a rationale; but, even accepting it, there are other case studies in hand. Take, for instance, Borussia Dortmund, still ahead of Bayern in the Bundesliga; or Athletic Bilbao who, while suffering in the domestic competition, have recently demolished ManU, creating and squandering lots of chances but still managing to comfortably prevail. These teams have no superior means to those of LFC; in fact, their means are far inferior, but they try to play good football to the best of their abilities.

Both teams also try, when in possession, to keep constant movement on the pitch: central defenders getting to midfield to create superiorities and facilitate passes and the finding of unmarked players; full backs constantly arriving at attacking positions to provide crosses or interchange of passes; midfielders going to one or the other wing to help opening the defences; wingers appearing sometimes inside the pitch, and other times in the wing; forwards looking for the weaknesses of the defences, and occupying the spaces when needed.

Well, obviously all this is just the objective, the aim. Very often, all the running leads to nothing, the ball is lost, and the players have to start it all again. But the mobility of the players is there for anyone to see. They try to attack that way. Sometimes they can; sometimes not. But the players, and the ball, are constantly running.

Says Marcelo Bielsa, manager of Athletic Bilbao: "I always say to the players that for us football is movement, that they need to be always running. For every player, in every circumstance, I find a reason to be running: in football there is no moment whatsoever in which a placer should stand still on the pitch".

I don't see this attitude in LFC players during recent matches. There are two main sources of movement in LFC: Suarez, who is constantly up and down, right to left, and vice versa; and Gerrard, who appears in opposition box, plays in the right wing, plays in the left wing, goes back to build the play,...But the rest of the team is mostly waiting for things to happen, and movement from two players is not enough. Two alternative sources of movement are Bellamy and Maxi. When played, they have showed a remarkable understanding with Suarez that is due, to a great extent, to that mobility.

That is not to say that the rest of the players don't run, don't work for the team. They do. But they tend to remain in their own areas of the pitch. That bodes well for defending: the players are seldom caught out of position. But it is bad for attacking. The big difference is that, in order to defend, you want to keep things calmed, to maintain the status quo. If nothing happens, you are not getting a goal scored against you. On the other hand, for your attack to be successful, you need things happening, the unexpected arriving, the situation changing. A lot of effort is needed to attack and to defend, but it is a different effort.

When a team starts to lack confidence, they are prone to stay put, to not lose position just in case something wrong happens. But to be the team that the fans, the players, and the staff want LFC to be, the players need to find a way to lose that prevention, and start trying more things on the pitch, more movements, more position losing, more risk taking. They may get more goals against while adjusting, but they might also not only score more goals, but also play better football. Or at least have more fun in the trying.

Eight league games, and one or two cup games, remain to be played, and the season is still very much alive. It still may end on a high if better performances are to be seen on the pitch.

39.- Walking through a storm

Date: 2-April-2012
Previous results: Newcastle 2-0 LFC (Premier League)

Yet another defeat, and LFC keep walking through a fiery storm in the League. And unexpectedly, given the moment in which this is happening; last December Suarez, arguably the most important player for LFC at the time, was banned for eight matches, which would have him out of the pitch during January. LFC managed to more or less navigate those weeks (League form: 1 win, 1 draw, 2 defeats), and on February 6th Suarez was available again. Apparently, the worst had passed, and the aim was to make amends for the points lost, and to look to the rest of the season targeting that all important 4th spot. Since then, the league results have been nothing short of a nightmare: 1 win, 1 draw, 6 defeats. Not only the 4th spot is well out of reach; even 6th looks unreachable, 7th the best possibility, and finishing in the second half of the table not totally impossible.

At this moment, everything seems to go against LFC, both deservedly and undeservedly. During this spell, LFC have had a well deserved victory against Everton, a draw in a good game against Tottenham, three more that deserved defeats in really badly played matches against ManU, Sunderland and Wigan, a really inexplicable defeat against QPR in a match totally dominated by LFC, an utterly undeserved defeat against Arsenal, and that last defeat against Newcastle.

Inevitably, such runs of games bring on the debate about "winning ugly". According to this theory, great teams need to develop a winning habit able to overcome the poorly played matches and win them. However, there is no way of planning a game with the aim of winning it through playing badly. All a team can do is to try to play as well as possible and try to convert that good playing into a win.

Which is what, I reckon, the team tried against Newcastle. The team entered the game really well. The first 20 minutes LFC played very well, nearly outplaying Newcastle. The only logic outcome of that was an LFC goal. In fact, a Carroll goal; Carroll was being absolutely superior to his opponents, and it seemed only a matter of time before all that dominance would lead to a goal. However, the team being through a storm, what came was a goal against.

During those 20 minutes, the team looked well. The defence, with the adjustment of playing Skrtel on the right and Carragher on the left, improved over last performances. Flanagan seemed solid and going forward very often, providing needed width in the attack. Jose Enrique, on the other hand, struggled with opposition and didn't add to the offensive. In midfield, Spearing swept every ball and conducted it well to the attacking midfielders. Gerrard linked well with his team-mates, though he did not quite get to his best. Shelvey looked omnipresent, helping Spearing, appearing on the right, on the left, linking with Carroll, with Suarez. Bellamy went time an again against his defender, beating him repeatedly and putting crosses on the box; unfortunately, his crossing was not accurate enough. Suarez moved freely, always targeting the best place to inflict damage. And Carroll offered his best minutes as a red, probably with the exception of his demolition of Man City last season.

To be precise, I am not implying this was a memorable football match or anything like that. It was nothing more (and nothing less) than well, nothing exceptional, playing. But it should have been enough to get the first goal of the match.

A first goal that went into the wrong goal, Reina's. A very well taken goal, preceded by a defensive mistake by Skrtel. From then on, the team never fully recovered, though until half-time kept an acceptable level, albeit not as high as in the beginning of the match. After half-time, the situation changed for the worse, and the team went back to previous matches, unable to dominate, and unable to create clear goal chances. The match never looked like an LFC goal was going to come. And it did not.

The second goal from Newcastle put in effect an end to the match. And to make things worse, it came the red card for Reina. Judging from television images, it is clear that the Newcastle player grossly overreacted, and Reina hardly even touched him. But the reaction by Reina is a good example of the level of frustration that the players feel. This match almost summarized that last spell of games as a whole: some good playing without reward, some indifferent playing, some poor playing, good actions unrewarded, mistakes hardly punished, and a final defeat.

Players' body language at the end of the match conveyed some sense of fatality, of things going bad no matter how well or badly they played, of acceptance of fate. It is not that they not run, or that they did not put effort into their game. These players have proved time and again his commitment. Only that they seem to have run out of ideas.

All LFC fans know well that, through a storm, one needs to hold his head up high and don't be afraid, knowing that at the end of it there are better times waiting. To a certain extent, this lesson applies to current situation of the team. To a certain extent, it does not. What I think is most needed by the players is to keep the hope in their hearts, the confidence in that the storm will end, and that at one point their effort and, overall, their good football actions, will get rewarded. The difference with the "storm" in the anthem is that the players should not simply wait for it to end, they need to take action and influx in the improvement.

This squad has not proved during the season to be as good as many expected it to be last August. Action will be needed next summer (and have no doubt started in offices) to dramatically improve the level and depth of the squad. But the players are much better than the results they are having over past two months. They need to regroup, stick to their strengths, follow the lines of the first minutes of the game against Newcastle, and end the season on a high, both in FA Cup and in the League. 7th place may not be a bright target, but LFC should never finish a season below that; in fact, even 7th is not a fitting objective. But, whether the players like it or not (most surely not), that is the challenge now; that is the challenge the team needs to affront in coming weeks.

No storm lasts forever, and much as LFC football dreams have been tossed and blown in the League season, there is still much to play for: FA Cup, good finishing in the Premier. And a whole new season, with fresh dreams and hopes, is waiting only a few months from now.

40.- A drop of golden sun

Date: 13-April-2012
Previous results: LFC 1-1 Aston Villa (Premier League); Blackburn 2-3 LFC (Premier League)

"A drop of golden sun", sang Maria in "The sound of music"; that, a glimpse of golden sun, even if just a tiny drop, was the feeling in LFC camp when Carroll, almost out of nowhere, headed home in injury time against Blackburn, to hand LFC only their third league win of 2012.

League results might seem to someone meaningless now, given that 7th is the better the team can achieve. But they are certainly not meaningless to me; there are a variety of objective reasons why they in fact mean. But, overall, a club that claims to be really great should aim to win everything it can. So every match matters: not the same, but matters.

I was certainly glad to see that header going into Blackburn goal, ending a rollercoaster of a match (though I must admit that until the final whistle came I was afraid of a late equaliser). The team did not play particularly well, and some mistakes were nearly embarrassing. But I think they showed some good signals.

They also showed some bad signals, though. To begin with, we have been told time and again that one of the problems was that, failing to score the first goal, the team played nervous, and that once that first goal was scored, everything would be better; then, the problem was the "bad luck" in scoring that second goal that was going to decide the match, and allow the players to play better.

Against Blackburn, the team found themselves 2-0 up after 20 minutes, and not having really done anything special. So all that remained was to quietly see the minutes passing, and maybe LFC scoring some more goals. And it should have been the case with a consistent team. But this LFC lack that consistency, and are very fragile. The two goals, and extra penalty, given away were mistakes that a normal, solid, team would have never made.

The good thing is the team was able to stop Blackburn almost completely in normal game, even when playing with 10 men. The bad thing is they all but offered the game to Blackburn, with those two penalties, and the set piece that ended in Yakubu's header. When facing a set piece against Blackburn, you should not leave unmarked any player; but if one player should not get unmarked in front of goal, he is Yakubu. Especially if you chose, as it was the case, to defend with every player on the pitch. That was very, very, bad defending, and could be extremely damaging against Everton, if repeated on Saturday.

But, as said above, there were also good signs. One was, of course, that "drop of golden sun" by Carroll at the end of the match. But, to get there, other things needed to happen. The defence scheme of the team (not only the back four) looked solid and capable of coping with the opposition players. Obviously, other than those three terrible mistakes. Agger can be seen improving almost by the minute, and hopefully he will be ready for the entire match in Saturday. Henderson played more than well as emergency right back. Spearing patrolled his zone convincingly, and tried to play the ball to red feet as much as possible. Shelvey showed some potentially opposition-destroying abilities, only that he did not appear as much as I would have wished.

Bellamy looked sharp, ready, smart in his movements, and a constant threat. Maxi proved that he cannot stop scoring, even after time in the bench. He is the single goal scoring threat from midfield, and should be much more used. He is the kind of player that is very difficult to read, both by his own fans, and, more importantly, by the opposition defenders. Finally, Carroll played very, very well under the circumstances.

Very often isolated up front, he run tirelessly, he kept the ball when possible, played it with accuracy, defended brilliantly when necessary, and scored the winning goal. Having said that, he showed even more potential that could be unearthed in an improved team. It was not the first time Carroll has displayed his qualities, but probably his most complete match. But he has to build upon it, and keep growing.

So, all in all, the match provided Dalglish with a pleasant headache in terms of team selection, with some not very often used players claiming their places for Saturday and the following games. Obviously, the not headache in goal is not pleasant at all, having to resort to the third goalkeeper. Jones didn't look very comfortable, which is nothing but normal, given not only the amount of time since his last competitive match but also everything he has gone through. But great matches often build unexpected heroes, so who knows?

Apart from individual performances, the team attitude was also better than in other matches. They not only fought and run as expected, but they didn't completely commit to defence, allowing some space for going forward and have some chance of winning the game. It eventually happened, but even if not, the team gave a good account to themselves.

That is, a good account given where they were coming from. Not a match that lives up to the expectations at LFC. But, at the very least, a drop of golden sun. Maybe just an insignificant and quickly passing drop in cloudy times; maybe a sign of what is going to come. Time will tell. And will start telling soon. Anyway, as the same Maria also sang, in the same song, LFC has "a long, long, way to run" ahead to get back where it belongs.

41.- A second drop

Date: 18-April-2012
Previous results: LFC 2-1 Everton (FA Cup)

Having labelled the winner against Blackburn as "a drop of golden sun", I am really lost for words now. Another last gasp winner, again by Andy Carroll, in a far more significant match. Nothing less than an FA Cup semi-final, in Wembley, against Everton, on the eve of Hillsborough anniversary,...A second drop, as it were, though certainly drops seldom come this big.

Whether these two important goals (yes, I keep thinking the Blackburn one was important, too) will provide the platform for Carroll to step up his contribution to LFC success and become a key player remains to be seen, but that is the hope in LFC camp. A commanding striker besides Suarez has been missing during the season, and Dalglish could use that partnership if goals and wins are found.

However, and as of now, Carroll and Suarez do not seem to really play well together, in terms of being more as a unit than each of them separately. Both played a big part in the victory last Saturday; but, each of them linked usually with other players. Carroll got two great crosses, from Downing and Bellamy; Suarez opted (and rightly so, given the outcome) to finalize himself in his goal; in stark contrast, it only took a 15 minutes appearance for Maxi to get a clear goal chance from Suarez.

All of this happened in one match, and could of course be just a coincidence. But in my view it is not. As have been often said, on paper, Suarez and Carroll have in them everything to form a formidable and terrorizing partnership, in the mould of Keegan/Toshack, Rush/Dalglish, Aldridge/Beardsley,... But, whatever the reason, that partnership has not developed in this first season. This is probably the reason why Dalglish is so hesitant to play them together. He is likely seeing something, both on matches and on training ground that prevents him from fielding the pair.

Those types of partnerships often develop almost instantly, as has been the case with Suarez/Maxi; that has not happened with Suarez/Carroll. But it is not impossible for it to develop slowly. And the fact that both started (and finished) the match on Saturday might be a good sign for the long term. Maybe Dalglish is seeing signs of improvement in their understanding; or maybe it is just a fan (me) looking for reasons for optimism. As with many other issues, time will tell.

But there was another tactical movement on Saturday I would like to talk about. I am not totally sure, because I was watching the match on TV and I may have been misled. But I am under the impression that, with Agger playing instead of Jose Enrique, Dalglish not only changed names; not only opted for certain type of left back over other type. He in fact tried a tactical change. And, if I am correct, it was not the first time that was put in place by an LFC manager.

There is a permanent dichotomy in world football between attack and defence; between going forward and keeping save the own goal; between searching a goal scored and preventing a goal conceded. While the football tactical richness allows for this dilemma to be assessed in many different ways, one of its manifestations is whether to play five defenders (typically in a 5-3-2 scheme) or four defenders (typically in a 4-4-2 scheme). As said, multiple other possibilities are possible, but those are two of the most used ones.

It was a problem particularly telling for LFC last Saturday, given the power of Everton in long balls and set pieces and the uncertainty about a goalkeeper almost untested in last years. So probably it was very tempting for LFC staff to go with five defenders, including three central defenders. The other side of the coin, of course, would have been to be weaker in attack.

And what I think I saw was that Dalglish tried to play a formally impossible "5-4-2" by playing Agger as central defender with Downing as left back when Everton were in possession and changing to Agger as left back and Downing as left wing when LFC had the ball. That was the situation, for example, in Everton goal, with Agger in the centre along Carragher, backing Skrtel. It might be the case that Agger simply went to the centre on certain occasions to help, but I got the impression that it was more than that. During long spells in the game, most notably after the Everton goal, that movement ended and the team played a more classical 4-4-2.

And that was not completely new. Benitez tried something similar in certain matches. It was usually Riise who was changing positions during games, between left back and central defender, or between left back and left wing. As far as I can remember, the second leg of 2004/05 Champions League quarter final against Juventus in Turin was the first (not the only) time in which that particular movement was put into place, with Riise and Traore as main characters.

I don't know. I might be reading too much into a much simpler situation. After all, paraphrasing Shankly, football "is terribly simple", and I might be complicating it unnecessarily.

Anyway, I think that that way of playing, moving your full back to the centre of defence to help the central defenders could be useful in certain situations. But it would take a lot of working in training to develop understanding between the players and to make the most of the possibilities. Otherwise, you could end up playing six defenders and emptying the midfield. And no one wants that.

At last, Shankly was most probably right about the simplicity of football. In that, understanding between the players, it being the strikers or the defenders, adds very much to the level of play. And Carroll "drops", in the form of last winners, will do him, and the team, the world of good if they keep coming, and help develop fruitful partnerships with his team mates. I look forward to the third drop of golden sun.

42.- Loyalty, pragmatism, fantasies

Date: 25-April-2012
Previous results: LFC 0-1 WBA (Premier League)

I should start this article by explaining that I am a regular Fantasy League player; I usually play both Premier League and Champions League Fantasy games. You know, those games in which you chose some players and score points depending on their performances. And I am not very good at those games. One close friend, who often plays with me, has repeatedly accused me of being too sentimental to really succeed at the game.

He undoubtedly has a point. At certain level of knowledge about football, the leagues, the players, the rules,...the way of playing the game have to balance two different approaches: the "loyal" players give every pre-eminence to their favourite players and teams; the "pragmatic" players only focus in the game, and only think about maximizing the points gained. My guess is that almost every player looks for, and finds, their particular middle point. Probably there is no player totally "loyal"; much players are somewhere in the middle; and there are some players that are totally "pragmatic", as my friend.

As he points out, I am biased towards the "loyalty" end. That approach has worked fairly well during past seasons, but is becoming increasingly difficult to maintain for an LFC fan. And, apparently, I happen to keep moving towards the "pragmatic" zone. Without really noticing it, really. At least, until this week.

Prior to last weekend matches, I decided to give a much needed global change to my team. So I went to the Transfer zone of the webpage, and started to buy and sell players. Once I was satisfied with the result, I confirmed the transfers and got ready for the matches to start and judge if I was right or wrong with my decisions.

And when I checked my team again, I realised that, for the first time since I play the game, there were no LFC players in it. Not a single one. That was not deliberate, but was clear to me. I had become a pragmatic, and was no longer the "romantic, loyal" player I was happy to be.

Probably that is a reflection of both, my own improved understanding of the game, and the disappointing league season by LFC. These types of games reward not exactly the good level of play by a player, but an easily measurable outcome of it. So, for example, Suarez (during most of the season not only one of my players, but in fact the captain of my team) got near to no points from his performance against WBA.

And I think he played an outstanding match. True, he didn't score, but he did every other thing that might possibly be asked from him. He ran, chased opposition players, looked for space, took the ball into the box, dribbled players, created all sorts of dangerous situations,...every thing except scoring.

This, to a certain extent, epitomizes what the team experienced last Sunday. I am the first to accept that the overall performance of the team in the league has been unacceptable. That said, the final score should not be the only aspect to judge. And in the WBA match I think that the team did more, much more in fact, than enough to win. That has happened at other moments this season (Arsenal home game comes to mind), but probably not as clearly.

It seemed almost impossible for LFC not to score, given the amount and clarity of the goal chances: from the right, from the left, from the middle, outside the box, inside the box, good shots, poor shots, saves by the goalkeeper, woodwork time and again,...To be perfectly honest, it was not that the team played extremely well; but it were extremely superior to WBA.

At the other end, Reina had only one save to make (a really good one, in the first time), apart from the goal that came after a mistake: a mistake caused by the ambition to keep on attacking quickly. Other than that, the defensive side of the team was very good; and that is not easy, when the team is on the attack all the time. But the defenders, with the remarkable help of Spearing and the rest of the midfield, prevented WBA from creating problems.

So, a good game, an elusive victory deserved but not achieved,...nothing to amend? Only bad luck to blame? Well, not quite, as I see it. On the one hand, the attack was very often confused, with lots of rebounds, the players rushing to the box,...without the sometimes needed pause and clarity of mind. It is one thing to create enough chances to have won the match; it is a different thing to really have attacked well. To sum up, attacking play was good, but with plenty of room for improvement.

On the other hand, after the WBA goal the team lacked reaction. They hardly created clear chances in those final fifteen minutes. While it is more than understandable for the players to be dispirited, the resilience is one thing the team could get from such a disappointing league season. The fighting spirit to keep going, "through the wind", "through the rain".

But at the end of the day, the score is LFC 0-1 WBA, and Suarez did not get many points in the Fantasy league. And, though I had not Suarez in my team, I didn't have a good week, either. Sometimes the "pragmatic" approach, even involuntary as in my case, does not guarantee any better results. Sometimes the "loyal" approach can be more rewarding, both in points and in personal satisfaction.

I have still to think about it, and decide my next movements in the Fantasy game. And I will be more than happy if LFC players get many points, whether or not I have them in my team. FA Cup final can only be well prepared by entering a good run of games and hopefully results. But it is more important to work on the level of play than on the results, I guess.

43.- Match and Cup lost; player and team gained?

Date: 7-May-2012
Previous results: Norwich 0-3 LFC (Premier League); LFC 0-1 Fulham (Premier League); Chelsea 2-1 LFC (FA Cup final)

A lot of football fans like to find a "defining moment", "turning point", "decisive crossroad",…in almost every match. At least I do. I am not talking here about moments that define a particular match, but moments that are decisive in the long (or at least middle) term, that change trajectories of teams or players.

Ultimately, experience teaches that there are not nearly as many turning points as we tend to think, and that most of the time we are reading far too much into simple facts. Real decisive moments are few and apart. And they might not even exist at all. But I prefer to think that they do exist, even if fewer than normally thought.

On the pitch, I still think that, for example, the dribble by Real Madrid player Redondo with his heel that led to a goal by Raul and Real Madrid knocking out ManU from 1999/2000 Champions League was one of those moments that changed the balance of power in European football for the following seasons. Or possibly Terry slipping during the penalty shoot-out in the 2008 Champions League final.

Off the pitch, there have also been some decisive moments, for the better or for the worse; Hillsborough, more than

Heysel, was probably one such moment for LFC. But I still think that points as defining are few. What I now wonder is: was there in last Saturday FA Cup final one of those moments? I can think of two candidates: on the one hand, Carroll scoring a goal; on the other hand, Carroll header saved by Cech (or being judged as saved).

Even knowing that, in all likelihood, neither of those will prove to be as decisive, there is still the possibility. Carroll's goal certainly changed the game. Up until that moment, as LFC players and coaches have admitted, LFC were second best. Not that Chelsea were playing particularly well; but LFC were playing as poorly as they come. No fighting spirit, no confidence, no damage to the opposition,…It was as if the players were playing nothing more than a pre-season match.

Had Chelsea been playing well, the match would have been well defined by the 60th minute. Still, 2-0 was, if possible, too generous for both teams; Chelsea were not deserving such lead (Reina had hardly anything to do, other than the goals), but at the same time LFC deserved to be out of the match.

Then Carroll entered the game, and shortly after that scored a very good goal. And everything changed. Chelsea defenders were unable to cope with him, and every LFC player stepped up their game. All of a sudden, there were red shirts everywhere. Chelsea were confined in their own half of the pitch, while LFC attacked endlessly. Not only much attack, but also very good attack at times.

LFC were able to be more dangerous for Cech than highly praised FC Barcelona. Only chance, Lady Luck, coincidence,...were to blame for LFC not getting an equaliser. And the real factor in it was Carroll; heading footballs, passing them to team mates, shooting at goal, dribbling,...A real definition of what "leading the attack" means. Up to now, we had seen glimpses of Carroll's game for LFC, but never at that level. Not even in the Man City match last season, in which he played very well.

So, one is tempted to think that maybe that match is a platform for Carroll to build on, and keep progressing to be the great player LFC thought to have signed. He not only played; he finally brought into play his team mates, and decisively stamped his authority on the match. As commanding a display as one can aspire to.

A performance that could have been crowned by a second goal. That might have led to an uncertain extra-time, and maybe made Carroll a total hero. It took a magnificent effort by Cech to stop that header that is surely haunting Carroll. Now, it is difficult to know which of those moments, the goal scored and the goal almost scored, will be more persistent in Carroll's mind. Focusing more on the not scored that on the scored goal could be the last nail in the coffin for his confidence as an LFC player, and the club members will no doubt do their best for avoiding it, and turning his mind to the goal scored and the performance changing.

Anyway, it is very well for LFC fans, and even LFC players, to keep thinking that during final 30 minutes of the final an equaliser was more than deserved; and it is arguably true.

But, for LFC staff, it is more compelling to think on the opening 60 minutes, in which the team was almost absent from the field.

Next season can be built on the final 30 minutes, with flowing attacking and efficient football; but too many times the team has performed as in the first 60 minutes, and that needs to be corrected. Either with signings, with tactical changes, with training ground work,...

Most likely, LFC and Carroll will have good and bad times from now, and this FA Cup final will not be seen as a turning point; but there is a chance that in years to come we will be able to look at this final and see it as the moment in which Carroll turned into a real LFC player, and the team found its way to facing and attacking top teams. In that case, the lost final could after all be a good investment in the future. It is never a good sign to lose a final; but if in the process you win a player and a team confident of playing, long term consolation might be there.

44.- Unfinished business

Date: 11-May-2012
Previous results: LFC 4-1 Chelsea (Premier League)

There is no hiding the disappointment of losing a final. But, if there was some possibility, one can think of few best ways than confronting the same team few days later. It is not the same, and both teams would have taken the FA Cup final with blind eyes, if given the choice. But it is better than nothing. Even more, LFC not only beat Chelsea but absolutely outplayed them during the length of the match. And that good result revealed an unfinished business, setting up a couple of challenges for the last game of the season.

It was a good final display of a season that has been far from good in Anfield (a total of 27 points out of a possible total of 57). It has been that home form that has decisively damaged the league campaign. Away games have not been perfect, but the total points achieved on those games would have been enough to reduce the gap on the top of the table teams, and make a more satisfactory league campaign. Not as expected from LFC, but not as poor as it has been. So it was good to end the season at Anfield on a high, both for the players and the fans, the club and the staff.

Not to forget Chelsea were not playing on all cylinders, LFC played a good game. Assured and composed in defence, and with some really good movements in attack. Some good attacking football, with a fairly good conversion rate. Overall, good news of the match included the participation of Agger *from*, rather than *as*, left back. I mean, Agger defended mostly as a left back. But when he supported the attack, he seldom did it running along the wing and crossing the ball; he more often advanced to midfield to help the passing and keeping of the ball. Being technically gifted, that role suits him very well, and can be used to the benefit of the team. A good idea for the future.

Other good news was the working of the central midfield pairing of Shelvey/Henderson. They managed to cope well with Chelsea midfielders, and create also danger when going into attack. Once more, Henderson proved to be of more use on the centre of the pitch than on the flank. Even so, he has not, as of now, delivered all that was expected from him when signed. Finally, the Suarez/Carroll partnership seems to be working better each time they get to the pitch. It has been difficult for them, but apparently they are improving their understanding. It has been one of the very few games in which both of them shone at the same time. More strikingly, the team scored four goals and both forwards played very well, but none of them scored.

On the minus side, another penalty missed. It is something that needs to be quickly addressed and solved. Adam, Gerrard, Suarez, Carroll, Kuyt, Downing have all missed at least one penalty during 11/12 season. Some of them somewhat irrelevant; some of them potentially decisive. Anyway, a solution is sorely, and urgently, needed on that front. It is surely a paradox that, in this context, the only title of the season was won on penalty shoot-out, but even then a couple of penalties were missed.

In the meantime, season is not totally finished. As I see it, at least two historical challenges are there for the game against Swansea. And that is apart from the general ambition of winning every game, and of finishing as high up the table as possible. Those arguments are more than enough to be highly motivated going into the last game of the season. And there is the feeling good factor of ending the season on high. So I absolutely agree with Dalglish when he says that there are plenty to play for, and I hope that the players will be up to expectations.

But there are two specific goals to achieve. On the one hand, the total points tally is now 52; the worst Premier League season has ended with 54 (1998/1999 season, a final 7th position). So this team could become the worst LFC Premier League team in terms of points; or could avoid it by winning the game. Not a pleasant challenge, but I for one would prefer to get to 55 points. On the other hand, there is the final position in the table. LFC have never finished below 8th, either in the Premier League or the former first division, since last relegation. Hence, never since Shankly took office have an LFC team achieved less than 8th league position. It would be hard to take, at least for me, to end up below.

Fixtures are on LFC side; there is a chance that even losing the game the team can finish at 8th place, if Tottenham beat Fulham. But it would be much better if the team could accomplish both missions: surpassing the 54 points tally and securing at least an 8th finish. Plus, by winning against Swansea the team would have the chance of bettering Everton and improving the league position. That is, "improving" until 7th place, which is not nearly good enough. But still.

After all, all those considerations are mainly meaningless. We fans want our team to win every match. We are more exciting with "important" matches; but we want to see our team winning even in completely irrelevant matches. Much more if the match is an official one, with points at stake, and the chance of finishing the season on a positive note. It is not a defining point in LFC history; next season will come with more significant challenges; but that is the unfinished business left in the season. That is the unfinished business I hope can be finished Sunday afternoon.

45.- End of a season, end of an era

Previous results: Swansea 1-0 LFC (Premier League)

The final game of 2011/2012 season put a somewhat predictable end to a league season that has been full of disappointments for LFC fans. After what was meanly an uneventful match that could have easily ended in a draw, there came a Swansea goal near the end of the game. So another defeat for LFC. Not exactly deserved, not exactly undeserved. The match might have ended 0-0, or 1-0 either way; but, as happened so many times in the season, the outcome was a 1-0 defeat. What I liked less was that it looked as if the players were not really motivated to avoid that ending to the season, looking pretty disengaged, as if the result was not important at all.

Such an ending meant that LFC totalled 52 points over the season, the lowest amount in its Premier League history, and arguably the worst tally since the last promotion to the then first division. Given that the system of awarding points changed, one could always argue that the teams would have played differently, so there is no straight comparison; but a close look to the total points amassed by LFC since that 1962-1963 leaves little doubt that 2011/2012 has been the worst league season in terms of points.

More than that, it has been only the third time since then that LFC have ended a league season in 8th place in the table. And never have an LFC team finalised below that in those seasons. So, from the point of view of sheer numbers,

2011/2012 has been the worst league season in the last 50 years for LFC. Fortunately enough, that season is now over.

However, it is not fair to draw such conclusions without further qualifications. As for the league, LFC are not playing now under the same circumstances as they were in the 70's and 80's, in which LFC had, comparatively, much better squad and more resources to compete; even so, let's not forget that, for 19 seasons running, since 1972-1973 to 1990-1991, the lower position, other than 5th in 1980-1981, was 2nd. So, who knows? Maybe that 5th spot in 1980/1981 could be considered more disappointing. I honestly don't know. But, to make amends, that season brought the third European Cup to Anfield cabinet.

What is clear is that, league wise, 2011/2012 has been a bad season, and no one in LFC is happy with that. It is true that maybe the final points tally does not accurately reflect what the team deserved. In very few, if any, matches, LFC got more than deserved; in more games LFC got less than deserved. Overall, the team could have easily won at least 8 or 10 more points. But that is part and parcel of football, and at the end of the season the final table is there for anyone to see.

But, seasons as a whole are not only about league. And, in Cup competitions, LFC have been almost perfect in 2011/2012. And, if only that header from Carroll in FA Cup final would have been goal, that "almost" might have had to go. LFC won the League Cup, having been drawn, amongst others, against Chelsea away and Man City over two legs in the way. So, it is not the case of an easy path to victory. It was a well won title, with the extra reward of finally getting a trophy in the new Wembley Stadium.

As for FA Cup, in order to get to the final LFC needed to beat ManU, Stoke, and Everton. Not an easy way, either. And every round was deservedly won. Admittedly, the final appeared too much of a challenge for the players for many minutes. Even so, the final moments are amongst the best LFC have played during the season.

When it comes to making a judgement about the season as a whole, I for one find it a nearly impossible task. A very poor league, an unbeatable League Cup, and a very good FA Cup. One piece of silverware after six years without titles. Three trips to Wembley. I would say that it has been a poor season, but not really a bad one. But the defining point has probably been that, overall, a if has been a season with little signs of the team progressing adequately for the future, which was, I reckon, the main aim last summer.

That is, probably, what has ultimately cost Dalglish his job. Hence, that last match of the season against Swansea marked not only the last match of Dalglish, but also illustrated the beginning of a new regime, a new era, given that, a few weeks later, the then manager of Swansea, Brendan Rodgers, was going to be unveiled as the new LFC manager.

After his departure, it is worth taking a look on this second spell of Dalglish as LFC manager. Only time will tell where the club will go from here, but as of now, the first conclusion, I think, is that the club is now in at least the same position, if not slightly better, as it was when Dalglish took the post in January 2011. That was a very difficult moment, with the club out of the League Cup, and in a poor run in the Premier League (25 points in 20 matches). On the other hand, the new owners were just arriving, so it is not easy to really know how would things have developed should Hodgson had remained in charge.

Anyway, that was a difficult moment, and Dalglish managed to steer the club out of it. One and half year later, the club have added one title and one FA Cup final, next year are going to take part in European competitions again, and league position is admittedly bad and inadmissible for LFC standards, but not terrible. However, there has been no clear progress in the league form. From those 25 points in 20 matches under Hodgson, the team went on to an estimable 34 points in 18 matches under Dalglish to finish the 2010/2011 season in a fairly good run; not title-winning, but at least near the best teams.

After a busy summer in the transfer market, expectations were the team was going to keep progressing. The first half of the league season showed no clear progress, with as many points (34) in 19 matches; but at least the team was showing good signs in the League Cup, so in that sense there was certain progress. However, the second half of the season was a different thing. 18 points in 19 matches is nothing short of relegation form. The League Cup title and FA Cup final are not enough to keep thinking that the team is on its way forward. And, as said before, this lack of perceived progress is what has probably determined the change of manager, not the judgement over a particular season.

This notwithstanding, Dalglish has completed a remarkable achievement, bringing the team back to Wembley, and winning the first title in six years. With that League Cup, Dalglish has won all English major titles (League, FA Cup, League Cup, Community Shield) both as a player and as a manager. His last spell as manager may have not been as brilliant as anyone, first of all himself, would have wished. But at least he has helped the team when needed, has got involved in a difficult moment, and has left the team in no worse conditions than he found it. Nothing to damage his long time held and extremely deserved status as Anfield legend and hero.

Now it is Brendan Rodgers' turn to try and steer the team forward. Much action, and many decisions, will need to be taken. First of all, he will need to be right with in the transfer market. Then, the management of the team, the tactics, the game plans, the type of play, the starting elevens and substitutions,...He has a complex and difficult task ahead. Anyway, he will have the support of the LFC fans, who will be hoping for a much improved season in 2012/2013, after a disappointing, yet eventful, interesting, roller-coaster, worth remembering, 2011/2012 course.

Printed in Great Britain
by Amazon.co.uk, Ltd.,
Marston Gate.